Please Upgrade For Access

How your ISP might be undermining your rights

Nate Levesque

Licensing

If you've acquired this book for free, please consider purchasing a copy to support the author. This is an independently published work.

Additional Information

The views expressed in this book are solely those of the author. They are not influenced by and do not reflect the views of any affiliations of the author other than by pure coincidence.

If at any point you find a factual error or poorly chosen source, you can make your concerns heard at www.natelevesque.com/factcheck.

~ ~ ~

Table of Contents

~ ~ ~

NET NEUTRALITY BRIEFING

1 · Net Neutrality

Rutherford B. Hayes, winner of the 1876 election, was not a likely president. He was obscure and was a nobody, let alone someone who could win an election. The eventual Republican candidate didn't receive the Republican nomination until the seventh ballot and was far behind the Democratic candidate. However, Hayes had the backing of Western Union and the Associated Press, two large companies interested in seeing him take office.

The companies had a partnership which gave them nearly exclusive control of breaking national and European news through the U.S. This control was possible because Western Union controlled the telegraph network, the only means of fast, long distance communication, and carried only reports from the Associated Press. Such control over the flow of news is hard to imagine today given the decentralized nature and variety of modern communication networks.

2

Western Union and the Associated Press decided to use their partnership to influence the election as Hayes had personal connections with them.

Through the election cycle, the two companies closely controlled what news went where about both candidates. Stories about Hayes that were positive were spread widely—such as stories about how honest he was—while stories of his scandals were kept in check. For the Democratic candidate, the reverse was true. This helped tip the election in Hayes' favor.

On the night of the election, the Republican party received word that the Democratic party was unsure they would win enough votes in the South for their candidate to win. Following that notice, the Republican party announced their own victory intentionally prematurely, causing a several month long electoral dispute. In the end, the Democratic candidate conceded, likely due to other deals of interest to the party to sweeten the concession, and Hayes was named president of the United States (Wu, 2012).

In 1876, communication was highly centralized around the telegraph network. Building the long distance lines that made the network national was an expensive job, one that could only be done by a powerful company like Western Union. There were no common carrier laws like those discussed as part of net neutrality so the company that built and ultimately owned such a network had total control of the data moving through it. The telephone, eventual successor to the telegraph, would later overtake Western Union's network under similar absolute control by Bell leading to the famous Bell breakup often referenced in the net neutrality discussion.

Communication in the 21st century looks very different. There are multiple networks which carry data in different ways and the telegraph is a distant memory. With the Internet, it seems all but impossible for a small number of companies to control the news—there seem to be too many places to get news and all are equally accessible. If you don't like one, you can choose another —the Internet makes that easy and if that's not good enough, radio, cable TV, and print media are all valid sources of information. Unfortunately, communication giants are still interested in control over what can be seen because if you control the information, you control the world and there are profits to be had from that.

When communication giants control enough of the networks people rely on, they become extraordinarily powerful companies which can only be reigned in by government intervention. Western Union had no such resistance during its election interference because neutrality in news and networks had yet to be considered. Its successor, Bell, prompted more attention and was broken apart. The companies that control access to the Internet have only recently begun to do things to be noticed in the same way but are good at lobbying and marketing. The public and the government have been convinced to look the other way with promises of free data and millions of dollars in lobbying.

Selling limits on what information can be accessed is surprisingly easy. Internet service providers have been doing it for years as fairness and quality assurance measures in the form of data caps and throttling. Content prioritization, or making certain information more accessible than others, is a little newer with the advent of practices like zero-rating—which comes with the appearance of getting free data access. Limits sometimes come with lower prices which can be appealing or even a necessity for those who are frugal or low-income.

Governments themselves, which one would hope have the best interests of an informed populace in mind, also have involvement in limiting access. This, too, is usually an easy sell. State censorship of the Internet is often passed into law under the guise of protecting something that everyone can agree should be protected while making opposition look like monsters. Protection of children, of morality, or of intellectual property—which most would agree are important—are some of the most frequent government reasons for limiting the Internet. Unfortunately, those laws tend to expand and become harmful, as has happened in countries like Turkey. Turkey's censorship laws were passed for such protection, but are now used as a general means of censoring the Internet.

While it would be a reasonable assumption that

practices limiting what people can access would prompt a public outcry or that legislation to prevent such limitations would be a priority, that hasn't been the case in the United States. Internet service provider (ISP) practices that limit the Internet don't have much to oppose them. Until its Title II classification, the Internet had few rules regarding what ISPs could do with it. First amendment rights to free speech do not cover ISP networks, only protection from the government when it comes to speaking out. This means that legally, ISPs may have the option to modify the messages they transmit to suit their views. While one would hope they wouldn't, there have been instances of service providers blocking certain content, however legal, from their networks. Usually, outcry has prompted them to change their mind. However, marketing has found ways to make these practices less obvious and more acceptable.

It's easy to think of ISPs as neutral providers of Internet connectivity, but that isn't necessarily true. They sit between you and a wealth of news and knowledge, with the ability to take control of what you can see. They're actively trying to sell you restrictions in the form of data caps and zero-rating, to convince you to pay less in exchange for less access. Your internet service provider having the ability to curate your world view in this way is highly worrying. If you follow the money and ownership of ISPs and media corporations, the idea of allowing an Internet provider to choose what sort of information your Internet package consists becomes an obvious problem. Internet providers now frequently own or are owned by the same companies that provide news and information that is generally expected to be correct and unbiased.

The following is the ownership of some larger news networks, based on information from "Who Owns The Media?," a resource provided by the Free Press organization, and an NPR breakdown of media companies and their many brands (Selyukh, 2016).

Comcast owns NBC, CNBC, and MSNBC.

Time Warner (not to be confused with Time Warner Cable), which is in talks to merge with AT&T, owns CNN.

Altice (Owner of Optimum) owns Newsday and AMC.

NewsCorp owns Fox and Dow Jones, as well as large stakes in several internet service providers.

This is far from an exhaustive list. Across the U.S. there are many media networks and internet service providers. Some don't own cable news networks but do own other media outlets. Verizon, for example, acquired print and digital media by buying AOL and happens to own the Huffington Post and several tech news sites. A recent acquisition of Yahoo gives the company control of question and answer sites, blogging services, and additional outlets.

Still other companies influence what information is available due to their size. Chances are, you've watched at least one thing created by Disney, Viacom, or 20th

Century Fox. These companies are so large that they can and do influence what's available to be seen and how you see it, not to mention having created much of it. A less obvious one is GE, which has stakes in NBC, SyFy, and Bravo among others. In all, as of 2012, about six companies controlled the majority of the media in the U.S. (Lutz, 2012).

You likely wouldn't get your news from the SyFy network (hopefully) so its ownership may not matter to you that much. However, you also probably wouldn't consider using Disney for your news network seeing as the company is best known for charming children's movies. What's interesting is you might unknowingly be doing just that. Disney owns ABC News, a news network, and ESPN, a sports network. Ownership of networks determines what ads are shown, which are intended by design to create or change your opinion of something so you'll be more inclined to buy it, to vote for it, or to support it.

This is, of course, not to make the claim that ISPs have any interest in manipulating what you see for political reasons. It is, however, worth pointing out that they may have the ability to do so. The last mile of Internet connectivity is not a healthy network when it comes to net neutrality because ISPs try to exert total control over the lines. In many cases, these same ISPs are also the gateway to what you can see on television because they provide cable services which are not required to be neutral. Internet and TV are the primary news sources in the United States, which puts those who have control over them in a position where they wield a lot of power if left unchecked.

Control over the lines is not limited to small coverage areas. Most service providers own large areas in which they may be the only provider or one of very few providers for reasonable service speeds. Acquisitions and mergers have made this problem worse by expanding control over networks in larger areas and possibly providing fewer options. Some ISPs may provide good quality service and reasonable prices, but not all do. Even the most benevolent ISP is a risk when they are the main carrier of information to a wide area. A large ISP may not be able to control information as Western Union did, but it may control enough to affect opinion if it so intended or by accident through prioritization of services willing to pay it.

Considering the limited number of cable and internet service providers in most areas, it's possible that your Internet and cable are provided by a company with opinions that differ from yours. If that's the case, switching to a different provider may not be possible because your ISP may be the only provider available to your house. On an Internet curated by your service provider, sites that provide views similar to your own might be suppressed in a variety of ways, many not at all obvious. If your viewpoint is more conservative you may even be more likely to see your views hidden, given the fact that most ISPs appear to be affiliated with networks that are regarded as more liberal or center.

Cable providers already drop channels from their lineups because of disputes between them and the providing network, usually over money and contracts. Without net neutrality there would likely be more of that, but not limited to cable. Online services could be subject to the same treatment. Netflix, for example, might become unusable because a service provider wanted to push their own streaming services. Facebook could become unavailable because it's not part of your Internet package. More nefariously, certain media outlets could become become irritatingly slow to access online because the service provider's own news networks were being prioritized in order to drown out competition in favor of more ad revenue or of different viewpoints.

This isn't as far fetched as it might sound. There are services like Google Fiber and Facebook Free Basics (formerly called Internet.org) run by Internet giants themselves trying to get started in the ISP business. Some of these services, including Facebook Free Basics, limit the Internet to a collection of websites curated by the provider so that users connected through them are subject to what the provider thinks they should be able to see.

Network infrastructure and media ownership at the forefront of net neutrality are not the only places where neutrality matters. Online services, especially those that serve a lot of people, can undermine net neutrality in other ways. Social media and other services curate what their users see and what they're able to do in a variety of ways. This normally manifests in the form of interest targeting—which is driven by user activity—rather than it does direct company actions. In similar fashion to ISPs, however, there have been instances of social media attempting to manipulate user views and emotions without users knowing.

The effects of these practices are wide reaching. They affect not only your access to information, but your ability to publish your own views whether you're an individual or a business. Most people experience the Internet as a source for information but the barrier to entry for becoming a creator is quite low. For under $20 a year it's possible to set up your own website and publish your own views and research to the world. A non-neutral Internet could be prone to sponsored droning out of small websites like your own similarly to how Walmart has had the effect of putting local businesses out of business. As an individual, competing with a huge online company to be seen online is near impossible on a neutral internet, let alone if that company has the support of ISPs. You, a small business, or an independent creator could be forced to choose which networks to be available on based on the fees imposed for being on them. A small local creator or business would be unlikely to be able to afford to be seen throughout the country.

Net neutrality protects people from the positions that

telecoms may hold by requiring them to not only allow you to publish and access other viewpoints from the carriers, but to allow you actually use the services providing those viewpoints by making sure you can get them at the same speed as anything else. Unfortunately, even with the current Title II classification, regulations may not be enough. In 2014, the FCC, the government agency that normally enforces such things, was stripped of much of its power to do so through its typical means. The FCC under Pai has stated that it intends to end net neutrality as soon as possible.

In the meantime, ISPs continue to get larger and more powerful, expanding their regional monopolies and lobbying abilities. Centralization is becoming more of a theme due to mergers and acquisitions which regulatory agencies don't appear keen to stop. Mergers like Time Warner Cable and Charter, two already large Internet and cable providers, to form Spectrum move the regional monopolies closer to national ones. Throughout the internet service provider industry, companies have been acquiring (and in some cases, re-acquiring) pieces of telecom infrastructure in extends that allow them to exert control over the Internet.

These activities are great for investors and the company bottom line, but not good for customers. As these companies get bigger and gain more control over what information people have access to it can start causing problems, in particular with how democracy works. The inability to verify news and to be correctly informed poses a huge risk to a democratic government. With the growing reliance on the Internet, a neutral Internet may be a necessity for democracy to continue to work as intended, rather than becoming a tool that telecoms can manipulate for their own needs.

Fortunately, most practices that undermine net neutrality are not problems with the Internet as a whole. The net neutrality fight is primarily about the practices of the last mile providers which serve mostly to deliver Internet to homes and businesses. Backbone providers, which connect wider areas between last mile providers, have more competition and are not responsible for most of the net neutrality concerns. Last mile providers, near monopolies in their areas, have not been truly restricted from taking advantage of the fact that they are the only option for getting online.

The protections required for net neutrality, as well as their implementations, differ depending who you talk to. The views expressed in this book—while in favor of net neutrality—are not the only possibility. As the Internet evolves and as ISPs find more ways to undermine net neutrality, views on how net neutrality needs to be preserved evolve as well. This book does not advocate for treating all network traffic equally—traffic prioritization is a necessary part of the modern Internet. This book is in favor of making sure the Internet remains equal and without prioritization or throttling of content so people can be informed and a company like the 1876 Western Union can't manipulate opinions.

2 · The Importance Of Neutrality

Just over 73% of households in the United States had a broadband Internet connection as of 2013 information from the U.S. Census Bureau American Community Survey Reports on computer and Internet use. The statistics of how many people lived in a household with a broadband Internet connection vary per state but at the lowest are around 62%. A whopping 78% of adults reported that they used the Internet, according to a 2014 Pew Research study (Rainie & D'Vera, 2014). That's a higher percentage of people online than people who have cable TV, which was at 68% as of the same year (Dugan, 2014). With the trend of cord-cutting, or canceling cable in favor of watching TV online, those numbers are poised to tip further to the Internet especially as live sports and traditionally cable networks such as HBO increasingly offer their own online streaming services.

It's unsurprising, then, that in 2016 almost a quarter of

people used the Internet to get their news, a number second only to cable and beating print media (Mitchell, Gottfried, Barthel, & Shearer, 2016). In theory, this is a positive thing because online, all manner of viewpoints and news outlets are available, including global ones. Accessing and weighing a wide variety of information from multiple sources to get to the truth is more possible now than at any other point in human history.

Unfortunately, the possibility of doing so and ease of doing so do not come together. While the opportunity to get information from multiple places is there, it's also easy to confirm your own viewpoint no matter what it is and no matter if it's correct or based in the real world. Many services now tailor the information they show to the interests of the person visiting them. Based on what the service you're using thinks you think, you'll see different ads, different stories, and different search results. Websites build a profile of you over time which they hope is accurate enough to tailor what they show. This is an imperfect science, but it's good enough that companies make a lot of money off of it. It's that money that allows free services to be free. The better the tailoring, the more time you'll spend on the website or so companies hope.

Two companies that do this are Google and Facebook. Google keeps track of everything you've searched for, every place you've visited, and many of the websites you've visited. It uses this information to power Google Now, its digital assistant, Google Adsense, its targeted advertising service, and to give better search suggestions. Facebook collects similar information based on pages "liked," the way of showing Facebook you're interested in something, as well as websites that use its "like" button, and posts made on its site. These influence the order of posts in its news feed, advertisements, and suggestions of other things that might interest you. Depending on the interests and beliefs the services think you have, they may present drastically different pictures of the world.

Typically, this type of targeting is done by algorithms which are trade secrets. While they are tweaked by humans—sometimes in ways that can cause obvious changes—computers are the ones deciding what lands in news feeds and suggestions. However, the same effect exists in discussion boards where real people choose to vote things up or down, determining what stays and what eventually disappears. Certain types of thinking might be more accepted than others on some sites. This causes some sites to develop a form of groupthink, where many of the users appear to have very similar views.

Reddit is one such site with a small amount of self-awareness of the phenomenon, which the Reddit community describes as "the hive mind." Most Redditors, as Reddit users refer to themselves, are fairly liberal. This in and of itself is fine, because Reddit provides a place where any discussion is welcome and it is reasonable to assume that the left leaning atmosphere isn't a product of Reddit itself but that Reddit is just the gathering place. However, certain subreddits, the smaller communities that make up the site, take great pain in censoring discussions. Dissent in those communities is unwelcome and results in users being banned from that community—even if the new ideas they introduce are reasonable and worth examining. Discussion and ideas can flow freely on the site only as long as they agree with the views of the hive mind. Anything too far outside those views is voted down by users until it effectively disappears. Reddit's resulting curated view of the world can be appealing and at times even quite useful, but using it alone would not provide a healthy world perspective. The ability and willingness to step outside the community is therefore incredibly important.

Unfortunately, interest targeting isn't always obvious and can even be welcome, as the Internet actively tries to make the world look like what you think it is. The effect is referred to as the filter bubble and can be dangerous with the percentage of people who get their news online. People relying on the Internet for information can slowly become separated from anything that does not confirm their own viewpoints. The effect can be isolating and divisive, and can have implications for public opinion and voting habits. Some, however, see the filter bubble as a minor problem which is repairable, although escaping the bubble requires active effort to seek out alternative services and viewpoints. It can also mean partially giving up certain niceties that come with a service knowing a lot about you, such as restaurant suggestions tailored to your tastes.

The online world doesn't end at social media and discussion boards. It's possible to get or to supplement an education online with free services such as Kahn Academy and even free college courses from top universities. Harvard is one such university which offers online courses, making it possible to attend lectures from the Ivy League school for free without even getting out of bed—albeit not for real college credit. Many colleges, including Harvard, use the Internet for their for-credit courses as well, using online services for assignments and grading. In an ideal world, this easy availability of educational resources could mean a more informed populace and a healthier democracy.

This further shows how important access to the whole Internet is. Without net neutrality, universities and question and answer sites could be forced to shutter their online learning services rather than pay ISPs to allow access to their content. It could mean your ISP could decide from what places you can get information, depending on your ability to pay. This introduces a digital divide—which could be even more difficult to compensate for than the filter bubble.

Indirectly, the Internet is used by far more than the 78% of people who report that they've used it. As a technology, the Internet is surprisingly pervasive. The majority of financial transactions that happen over the course of a day are powered by the Internet. Credit, debit, and even check transactions enter into their respective payment networks via the Internet from many retailers. Stripe, one of the most well-known online payment gateways, is used by over 100,000 businesses and handles billions of dollars a year according to its company website. Stripe processes credit card, Bitcoin, and ACH payments for all sorts of online services such as Reddit and Facebook as well as for traditionally brick and mortar retailers such as Target and Best Buy.

In addition to payments, banking, health, and ownership records are often securely passed over the Internet to make sure they're available where you are and to ensure they won't get lost due to computer problems. This allows your primary healthcare provider to send your medical history to the provider caring for you in an emergency, for instance, or to move your records to a new provider when you switch. It also means you can access your bank account at any ATM or branch anywhere in the world with up-to-date balances and transaction records. Finally, it keeps your data safe. In the event of a disaster, data are pulled back from the cloud or from a remote location to make it available again. Due to this, you may not use your bank's online portal, for example, but your bank is most likely moving your information over the Internet anyway. Your data can be replicated across the country almost immediately so should your local bank branch, hospital, or what-have-you suffer a computer disaster, nothing you own and nothing about you is lost.

Various other services you may use rely on the Internet as well. Cable TV, which is often provided by the same companies who provide Internet access, uses the same infrastructure as the Internet. Telephone calls over certain phone networks, particularly wireless, are routed through the Internet. The technologies that make the Internet possible are flexible and present almost everywhere, which makes it convenient to use them for more than just the public Internet.

All of these services rely on an open Internet to serve their customers, and in some cases, to serve their customers' customers. Businesses are free to choose if they want to process payments with Stripe or an alternative company without their ISP being involved in the decision, for an example. This has real repercussions for the people they serve—businesses have the freedom to move to a different payment processor if there's a security breach, for instance. It also means those business are free to set up shop anywhere they want, without needing to worry about whether the available ISP allows them to continue their normal operation.

The freedom to choose and the ability to be informed are at stake with net neutrality. Nearly everyone is using the Internet in some form, knowingly or not. The assurance that that usage will not be impacted by ISP practices is important. If it is, privilege gaps could appear. What and where information can come from could change depending on where you are. How well businesses can serve customers could change depending on their ISP. Where your information can come from and go to, so long as it's legal, is not something your Internet provider should have a say in.

. . .

3 · But It Was Paid For

One of the more frustrating aspects of Internet infrastructure in the U.S. and ISP policies around it is that large parts of it were funded by the public. While ISPs currently own and operate the infrastructure, not all of the funding that went into building it was invested by the companies themselves.

As with other infrastructure projects, expansion and upgrading of Internet infrastructure have been funded by taxpayer dollars. At a high level, this is fine because Internet is a critical service in the modern world. Ensuring networks are up to modern standards is necessary for providing access to information, education, and other services. However, the network improvements expected from many of these grants have never materialized. There are still people in the U.S. who do not have Internet speeds available to them that are usable for accessing modern websites.

Net neutrality or not, ISPs have a rocky past with regard

to keeping promises of network improvements. Service providers have on numerous occasions reneged on promises—even promises that were already funded by taxpayer money—to improve their networks. Other times, they made a show of implementing those promises only for taxpayers to later discover that they did not get their money's worth.

In New York, New Jersey, and Pennsylvania, a large, national ISP promised expansions to its fiber network in return for government subsidies and benefits. The expansions would have provided Internet to millions more people and would have improved the speed of service for others. However, while the government benefits were provided at massive taxpayer expense, expansion of the network was never completed. Instead, the ISP attempted to convince local governments that unfinished expansions and non-viable alternatives to its network met the terms of its agreements.

In New Jersey, the company had its employees help it convince the New Jersey Board of Public Utilities that DSL and the ISP's LTE network qualified for meeting the terms of its agreement (Masnick, 2014). The company was, as a result, accused of astroturfing, or attempting to make the appearance of a show of support for itself using manufactured personas—in this case, its employees. The ISP's argument that the two alternatives covered where its fiber network did not was not entirely true—the alternatives provided Internet, but not at anywhere near the same quality. LTE service from any wireless carrier is expensive, has data caps, and compared to fiber is extremely slow. It does not in any way compare to a wired home Internet connection and is, even in 2017 with 5G networks on the horizon, difficult to impossible to use as a primary connection. DSL is also a significantly slower technology than fiber, with upper limits on speed due to limits of the technology. The New Jersey Board of Public Utilities, convinced by the ISP's efforts, agreed that LTE and DSL covered the remainder of the contract. The board reported by agreeing with the stance, New Jersey taxpayers were saved the expense of years of litigation. However, taxpayers were still left having paid for improvements that were promised, but were never delivered.

The company argued in New York City that the terms of the agreement did not require it to actually connect anything to the fiber it did install, just that the company needed to run fiber down the street in front (Masnick, 2014). For taxpayers whose money ultimately funded the project, that meant although they paid for fiber Internet service to be expanded to schools, libraries, and in some cases themselves, they got no return for their money. Homes and public facilities that wanted access needed to pay the ISP a second time to actually connect them to the network, even though the original intent of the contract was that the company would connect them as part of the construction.

In West Virginia, taxpayer-funded improvements to

infrastructure actually made the Internet worse. Before work began, West Virginia ranked 48th out of 53 (including U.S. outlying islands) for Internet access, almost last in the country. The state provided funding to a network operator for network improvements that would, according to the agreement, provide a network that would allow for more provider options and provide service to some 700,000 homes and over 100,000 businesses. Unfortunately, the ISP did not deliver.

As a result, the ISP was accused of misusing $40 million dollars of federal funds. Lawsuits from 2014 allege that it had billed for almost double the fiber than was actually installed. At the same time, it allegedly inflated installation prices by overcharging for administrative activities and vehicles, in amounts that were at times more expensive than the construction itself. Even worse, additional lawsuits allege that the company used federal funding to further its monopoly on Internet service by expanding its own last mile network to homes and businesses, while the intent of the funding was to build a shared network for multiple ISPs. The upgrades cut competition so much and expanded Internet access so little that after the expansion project was completed, West Virginia ranked even worse for Internet access, at 53rd (Bode, 2016).

In all, the U.S. has spent some $400 billion to deploy fiber broadband connectivity throughout the country (Kushnick, 2015). Even with these hundreds of billions of dollars in government help to improve networks, ISPs still allege that they need to raise prices, cap and throttle data, and sell Internet similarly to cable. The fact that Internet providers can't be held even to promises they made to local and federal governments underscores the need for better regulation and net neutrality. Taxpayers have individually paid thousands of dollars for Internet service improvements that have never happened, not to mention money spent directly paying for Internet service.

This is not to say that the government should not offer grants to ISPs to expand their networks. When used as intended these grants help improve Internet service to rural and low-income areas that large, well-known ISPs are less interested in providing service in because of smaller profit margins. These grants can benefit the Internet as a whole as well. In Alaska, grants were used to prepare the network of the Arctic Slope Telephone Association Cooperative for the construction of another undersea cable to link North America with Europe (2015 Community Connect Broadband, 2015).

Municipal networks are another valuable result of grants and taxpayer money. These networks tend to provide better service and better prices as opposed to most large ISPs. Funding provided to such networks is also easier to track and to have an impact on because the companies behind them are usually local and answer to the communities they're in.

ISPs have argued that they will keep their promises if the regulatory schemes they support come to pass. This is offensive, given the billions in taxpayer funding provided to them for the purpose of doing just that. The problem with the ISP argument that network improvements will come with a non-neutral Internet is that until recently, there has been little with regard to enforcement of net neutrality regulations. In fact, ISPs are now running ads against net neutrality that push for the regulations that were in place when they first made the claim.

In early 2016, the United States ranked 16th in average Internet speeds ranked by Akamai (a huge cloud services provider) (Akamai's [state of the Internet], 2016) with some of the highest costs of service in the world. Ranking 16th in and of itself isn't actually terribly bad and Akamai's reports show that speeds are improving. However, with a several hundred billion dollar investment in broadband infrastructure, the ranking could be better.

Service could also be available for a much more accessible price. The fact that taxpayers have fronted such an enormous part of the cost of networks run by telecoms makes it hard to justify such high costs of service. Internet service in France is about three times cheaper and in South Korea was five times cheaper for high speeds as of 2013 numbers (Geoghegan, 2013). It's worth noting that competition in broadband Internet service is much better in other countries, which is a likely factor for better prices. However, telecoms often claim that practices that raise the cost of data are covering the cost of maintaining networks, despite receiving large sums already.

Unfortunately, taxpayers will likely continue to pay for broken promises. Enforcement of agreements for taxpayer money have been lax and easily overcome by ISPs, such as the case with New Jersey. The FCC under Pai appears unlikely to be interested in enforcing agreements made with ISPs for expanding their networks. This makes the claim that ISP customers and upstream providers should pay more for their usage or put up with limited access plans almost offensive.

Net neutrality regulations that encourage competition and transparency should help with these issues. Parts of the investment in broadband infrastructure have actually improved networks, though in many cases not access to them. Ensuring that funding intended for infrastructure is used correctly and provides the benefits promised is much easier when direct regulations can be cited. Making sure that the networks can actually be used once they're built—as some networks have been lobbied out of public use—is another side of it. Regardless, taxpayer funded infrastructure should benefit taxpayers in some form, not just the bottom line of the companies that built it.

* * *

4 · Networks Without Neutrality

It's difficult to know exactly the form a non neutral Internet might take. While ISPs have stated that they are committed to an open and unfettered internet, practices that they employ bring that statement into question. Zero-rating, data caps, and other questionable practices show the possibility of the first cracks in a neutral internet. Looking at ISP practices and state-sponsored policies from around the world provide examples of what a non neutral internet might entail.

Although the net neutrality situation in the UK has improved since, UK laws used to allow broadband Internet providers to impose any limits on Internet connections they wanted, as long as they were transparent about what those limits were. In 2009, some UK providers took advantage of those laws to develop heavily restricted Internet packages. One major provider, BT, slowed down things including streaming video, much to the annoyance of the BBC which had a new streaming service in place for streaming BBC shows online. BT also throttled other services and capped data and speeds of what it classified as "heavy users." There were three plans BT offered to customers. The first allowed 10GB per month of data use with restrictive throttling. It also limited monthly video streaming, even within the imposed data caps, something that could make Netflix or Hulu unusable. The second plan had 20GB of data allowed, still with heavy usage throttling. The third was an unlimited plan which still included throttling for "heavy use" (Anderson, 2009). Of course, with a better plan came a higher monthly cost. The alternative was to switch to another service provider, which in the UK was less of a problem than it is in the U.S. because the UK has much more competition when it comes to Internet service.

Other than the unlimited plan, the plans offered by BT would not have provided enough data for the average U.S. household in 2012 based on the fact that the average monthly use that year was 52GB (Lardinois, 2012). The limits would likely have made services such as Netflix a rarity due to the limits and throttling of streaming video.

China, which is well-known for its heavily restricted Internet, is another demonstration of a non-neutral Internet. Internet users in China are separated from the rest of the world by what's known colloquially as "The Great Firewall of China" which as of 2015 blocked access to some 3,000 websites according to a count on

Wikipedia. The list of blocked websites at times included Google, Yahoo, and Twitter as well as a variety of news sites and other services. Websites that criticize the Chinese government or its censorship policies or that mention things like Tiananmen are usually blocked automatically based on their content. What can make these restrictions more frustrating is that certain sites are sometimes allowed and other times are not based on where in China you happen to be and on current events in the world.

In order to provide a relatively modern Internet, there are state-sponsored social media sites as alternatives to the Facebook and Twitter of the rest of the world. While The Great Firewall of China makes it difficult to access a lot of information that the Chinese government deems distasteful, it isn't perfect. Using services such as VPN—which have been blocked on and off as well—it is possible to access websites that are blocked. However, doing so can attract the attention of authorities.

Turkey has policies for state sponsored Internet censorship that rival China's. A 2007 law gives the government authority to censor and block websites under the guise of protecting minors and families (Akgül, 2015). These laws and the government agency created to handle that censorship have since been used for far more than protection of minors and families. Bans, some implemented, some not, and some temporary have included YouTube, Facebook, Twitter, Wordpress and Blogger (blogging websites), as well as others less familiar to those in the U.S. but widely used abroad. Most recently, at the end of April 2017, Turkey began blocking Wikipedia, a community-maintained online encyclopedia. It doesn't take a lot of effort to get a website blocked in the country. One website, which denounced anti-evolution claims written by a Turkish author, was blocked for a time for "defamation." ISPs in Turkey that do not implement these bans are subject to government intervention, including incarceration of those in the company. At the end of 2008, only 10% of the blocked websites were blocked for child protection reasons. Censorship of websites in Turkey has even gone so far as police raids on individuals who were caught accessing censored services.

China and Turkey are somewhat extreme examples when juxtaposed with the United States. In the U.S., it's unlikely that websites would be all-out blocked on a non-neutral Internet. In particular, due to freedom of speech and freedom of the press guaranteed by the Constitution, it's extremely unlikely that there would be widespread state-sponsored censorship of the Internet. However, service providers can encourage the use of certain services over others through data caps and zero-rating or by selling tiered access to sections of the Internet. The technology exists to split access to the Internet like this, and not only based on websites. ISPs could block only specific pages that cover information not included in your Internet plan.

U.S. based ISPs already provide limited Internet

services that do exactly that. Facebook Free Basics, formerly called Internet.org, is one such service that has been in the news because it was recently banned from operating in India. The company suggests that it's helping the developing world by providing free access to the Internet to people who can't otherwise afford it. However, Free Basics is far less noble (Elgan, 2016). The service provides access to Facebook and a small curated collection of services and websites. Anything outside that list is not available. What's worse, is that millions of users of Facebook Free Basics are not aware and don't have the ability to discover that there is an Internet outside that list (Mirani, 2015). They believe that Facebook is the Internet. Facebook claims that Free Basics users eventually upgrade to a normal Internet package. Not all do, however, and having access only to a curated collection of sites does not make the full set of opportunities available to those on the limited plan. For users who are unable to afford better service, Free Basics is not a path to a full Internet plan but a sort of Internet slum that they're unable to escape.

In fairness to Facebook, its Free Basics program has been updated to allow submissions of sites not already included in it. As long as sites meet a list of guidelines, they can be included in the program regardless of their content. The requirements are technical and essentially require sites to limit their bandwidth use so as not to overload the network, and to limit some of the technologies they use in order to work on older phones. This is an improvement, but still makes the service a non neutral network with a barrier to entry for any company or individual wanting to be seen on the network.

Other Internet services with a free tier such as Google Fiber have yet to directly do anything against net neutrality, but in a non-neutral Internet would be within their rights to offer the same type of curated service. Google Fiber sends traffic over a network operated by Google. Google also provides a variety of its own online services which are widely used. The company for a time was considering providing its own solution to Internet access in underserved areas using drones, which could be a positive thing, but if limits were imposed unequally, would be another non neutral network.

The problem with these curated networks is that they are not the Internet. While they provide some access to the Internet to people unable to afford it, they lack the basic freedom of information and opportunity that makes the web so valuable. Providing even capped access to the Internet is a good thing, so long as those caps or other limitations are applied equally to the entire Internet, not just to certain services. Adding limits to what parts of the Internet can be accessed is the problem and is what makes non neutral services like Facebook Free Basics a problem. Two-thirds of the world still don't have easy access to the Internet, but limiting them to only part of it—and especially convincing them, accidentally or not, that that is the whole Internet—is problematic.

Despite claims to the contrary, mainstream Internet providers have already started to do this. While Facebook Free Basics does not operate in the United States, other big-name ISPs have been implicated in similar practices. Several have been named in multiple net neutrality lawsuits for encouraging the use of their own services over others. Zero-rating, throttling, and blocking high bandwidth applications are further steps towards a more restricted Internet and are all things that ISPs are slowly putting in place.

The FCC has allowed lawsuits about those practices to move forward in the past, which shows support for a neutral Internet. Unfortunately, the FCC under Pai no longer appears interested in protecting customers from those sorts of practices. Congress itself has introduced its own censorship bills, SOPA and CISA, for censoring certain Internet traffic in the U.S. Even more recently, a bill called the "Restoring Internet Freedom Act" was introduced which would remove the Title II regulations put in place in 2015 should the FCC not do that itself. Given the opportunity, ISPs would, of course, find profit in selling only parts of the Internet in bundles, to much the same effect. In all cases, there is profit and power to be found in controlling access to content. The challenge is finding the marketing to do so in order to avoid attracting the ire of the public and of advocacy groups.

Ensuring that access to the Internet means access to the whole Internet is paramount, especially as companies look to low-income and underserved areas as their next network expansions. The Internet was never intended to be a place of class-based opportunities and indeed, allows opportunity to be found in all walks of life. Global examples of restricted access already exist; net neutrality hopes to prevent local ISPs from following in those footsteps.

. . .

THE NET NEUTRALITY DISCUSSION

5 · Free Speech

Freedom of speech and freedom of expression are core values of the open Internet. Online services give everyone access to platforms through which they can share their views and make their voices heard. With over 1.2 billion people sharing their voices on Facebook alone (according to statistics Facebook published in early 2017)—not to mention other social networks and websites—it's clear that the Internet has made speaking up more possible than ever before. However, Internet providers appear to think that an Internet without such freedoms is more profitable, preferring to make some voices a little louder than others.

In 2012, a large internet service provider and mobile carrier filed a brief with the U.S. Court of Appeals opposing net neutrality regulations from the FCC. The company claimed that the FCC did not have the authority to regulate its service as the FCC was trying and that even if it did, the net neutrality regulations would be in violation of the company's constitutional rights (Lee, 2012). Essentially, the ISP was claiming it should have the same ability to manipulate content passing through its network as a newspaper editor had over what appeared in a newspaper. The company went on to claim that net neutrality was somewhat of a regulatory theft of its network, a Fifth Amendment problem.

A small ISP outside San Antonio, Texas followed suit in 2015 with a similar brief (Brodkin, 2015). The ISP claimed, similarly, that net neutrality prevented it from sending a message by prioritizing and speeding up some websites over others. The filing says, "by foreclosing prioritization, the Order restricts broadband providers' editorial discretion to favor their own and unaffiliated Internet content." The claim effectively says that your ISP should be allowed to give priority—through fast lanes, zero-rating, or by other means—to its own services and services it has agreements with to send its own message.

AT&T, CenturyLink, CTIA-The Wireless Association, and the United States Telecom Association made the same First and Fifth Amendment claims in between the two filings. These claims have not held up in court, with a precedent in 1994 which said that rules requiring telecoms to carry but not modify content over their networks were not unconstitutional (Lee, 2012).

The issue with service providers exercising supposed free speech rights to curate the online world is that it can stifle the rights to freedom of speech of everyone else. The fact that an ISP would argue that it should be able to provide an editorialized version of the Internet is concerning. As it is, the Internet is a big place and expressing your own views can at times feel like screaming into a crowd. That's with an internet that is neutral—there will always be others, and there will likely always be sites larger than yours. It's even worse considering the close relationships telecoms often have with media outlets. With ISP-curated Internet access, your voice isn't just hard to hear, it may not exist at all. Paying for access to the Internet should not subject you to the whims of the service provider you have access to.

The stifling of voices online goes beyond social media posts and personal blogs. Without a neutral Internet, independent creators would be far less able to find access to an audience. The digital realm gives "Indie" creators the ability to sell creations globally without the support of other companies. This is a big deal because it has allowed the Indie community to expand, becoming far less niche than it is in the offline world. Without the help of the neutral playing field online, published works would be limited to those that got accepted to large publishers and those from independent creators who got lucky. The neutral Internet empowers people who want to forge their own way. Whatever it is that you create or hope to create, you can find an audience online.

Pushing out individual and independent creators is far

from unprecedented in the evolution of information technologies. Radio experienced a similar problem, though when it came under government regulation as opposed to before. The Federal Radio Commission (FRC), the precursor to the FCC, was formed in order to regulate radio. Prior to the FRC, radio was composed primarily of independent local stations, with few if any national ones. The FRC fundamentally changed how radio stations were distributed to transform radio into what it is today. Regulations made the majority of the radio spectrum large, national stations and left little room for independent local stations (Wu, 2012). Whether or not this was the right approach has room for some debate. Radio went from a place of wide local opportunities and independent stations to a crowded space dominated by companies such as iHeartMedia which owns some 830 stations across the country.

Cable TV suffers from a similar problem. Cable is a place where the neutrality battle was fought and lost, so it is not a place where everyone has an equal chance. Independent creators have a difficult time being seen unless they are picked up by a larger network (and are then no longer independent). The problem largely stems from channel bundling, the selling of groups of channels together, which forces carriers to buy and air multiple channels together. Bundling is the reason that when you subscribe to cable, you get a variety of networks from the same distribution company. Since bundling became a standard practice, channel bundles have grown to 65 or more channels in some cases—

which leaves little room for independent creators. Indeed, Indie networks—and, interestingly, small cable companies—asked the FCC in early 2017 to stop the practice of bundling to help make cable a slightly more open playing field (Cox, 2017).

The Internet itself is not perfect with regard to net neutrality and being heard. There already are forms of fast lanes and incentives for using certain services. Companies such as Netflix have agreements with service providers so they can place servers on ISP networks, something Netflix discussed on its blog in 2016 (How Netflix Works With ISPs, 2016). Netflix's agreements place it closer to its users and allow it to deliver streaming video faster and at higher qualities than its competition.

Practices like these give an edge to the services that are able to benefit from them while making it harder to be independent. Netflix, for example, has become a content creator itself, churning out original series with great success. By also being its own distributor, Netflix doesn't need to worry about making deals with television networks or other content distributors to push its content to an audience. Netflix can, however, drone out competitors and independent creators with its standing. Indeed, Netflix, often cited as a net neutrality advocate, left the fight for net neutrality explaining "we're big enough to get the deals we want" (Bohn, 2017).

Though Netflix later retracted what it said, the

statement illustrates the issue of large companies being unconcerned about net neutrality. While some are in favor of net neutrality, or some are making the appearance that they are, a non neutral Internet prevents independent competition from digging into their bottom line. While Google, for example, may claim to support net neutrality, the company has little to lose if net neutrality is overturned. Indeed, Google appears to be making minimal efforts to support the cause (Schatz, 2014). Large services and content providers can afford agreements with ISPs to provide better access to their services. Startups and independent creators could be shut out entirely from certain parts of their audience should large creators begin to negotiate exclusive arrangements with ISPs.

ISPs themselves have attempted to exert control over free speech. In 2007, a major carrier blocked a pro-choice organization from sending text messages to its supporters. While it's unclear whether the action was politically motivated or did directly adhere to company policies, the carrier was the only mobile provider that chose not to allow the activist organization to send these messages. Outcry from all parts of the political spectrum as well as from organizations on both sides of the issue drove the carrier to back down from its stance and allow the campaign to continue. The company claimed that blocking the messages from its network had nothing to do with the political opinions of the company, but that it simply didn't allow politically charged messages to be sent en masse (Liptak, 2007).

However, SMS messages are not free so the carrier was forgoing collection of those fees to block the messaging, which raises further questions.

With the blocking of political text messages in 2007, legal experts noted that SMS was a service which carriers were likely allowed to discriminate on. As SMS is often used for political activism, blocking that type of messages can begin to tread into interference with political activism. SMS is only tangentially related to the net neutrality discussion. However, the same discrimination rights carriers had over SMS messages likely apply to the Internet as well. There is no established line for ISPs and mobile carriers allowing political activism on their networks. Blocking such messaging equally is less of a problem than blocking it selectively, but still treads into some grey areas in free speech.

In 2007, the whole political spectrum opposed the blocking of SMS activism from the pro-choice organization. Since then, politics in the U.S. have become much more divided and much more competitive, so the outcry from similar actions might not be enough to push companies to do the right thing. It's easy to brush off activities that work to quell speech you don't agree with, but far harder to support the general right to free speech when it includes opinions you find distasteful.

Net neutrality regulations aim to make sure ISPs are not able to limit freedom of speech online. The Internet is a very different technology than radio or television, with much more room for more voices and companies, having the advantage of no limitations on channels. Internet providers would prefer to put in place policies that increase revenue—even at the cost of making their customers less informed. Large companies would have the leverage and the funding to make deals with ISPs to be seen better than the local alternatives. Big business would take control, while you, local businesses, and Indie creators would be shut out.

. . .

6 · Curated News

The Internet offers the possibility of visiting any news network from around the world, with automated translation services so they're available in any language. Should you want to, you can peruse the Russian front page alongside the New York Times, alongside Fox News. While regularly browsing the front page of Russia's newspapers is likely to get you on one of the rumored intelligence agency watch lists, nobody can stop you from taking a peek, least of all your ISP—as long as the Internet is neutral.

It turns out that a lot of people take advantage of the opportunity to get their news online. Almost 40% of Americans got news from online sources according to a Pew Research study in 2016, making the Internet a news source second only to television (Matsa & Lu, 2016). The number is likely to continue to grow as the trend of cord cutting continues and satisfaction in cable companies continues to fall. This underscores the importance of having an Internet in which the company you access the Internet through can't manipulate what you see.

Given the opportunity to control such a powerful and widely used medium, ISPs and upstream providers likely will find profit in doing so. Even if they don't go so far as to outright block things, they are able to slow sites down or make them harder to access. It is unlikely that an ISP would be able to render websites totally unreachable without incurring expensive court battles and public outcry. However, deterring people from visiting a website takes very little and can go unnoticed. Even delays too small to be noticed on a conscious level will push people away from using those websites. Slowing down a website by roughly a blink of an eye is enough to push visitors to a competing site (Lohr, 2012).

Control over the news, especially with regard to net neutrality, is something ISPs are already engaging in with close relationships to media outlets as well as with threats of legal action. A firm contracted by Comcast, for example, sent a cease and desist letter for copyright infringement in 2017 to a website called comcastroturf.com, the name of which is protected under fair use. The website attempted to provide insight into people being impersonated for the purpose of leaving anti net neutrality feedback on the FCC's net neutrality proceedings (Fight For The Future, 2017). Without net neutrality, an ISP could block or throttle the site rather than sending questionable cease and desist letters. Comcast stated the letter was sent unintentionally by the contracted firm.

ISPs slowing down certain traffic on their networks to push people to other services is not unprecedented either. In 2008, a service provider was caught trying to secretly slow down BitTorrent, a peer to peer file sharing service, in an effort some believe was intended to encourage the use of the service provider's services instead (McCullagh, 2008). In 2014, Netflix ran into a similar battle where slower speeds on the same ISP's network were causing Netflix subscribers to switch to other services (Goldman, 2014).

The problem isn't limited to speeds. Practices such as zero-rating also provide a push for ISP customers to use one service or news network over another. By exempting certain sites from data caps, ISPs can sell what sounds like free data while nudging their customers to use what the ISP zero-rates.

Social media sites can have the same problems. A majority of adults—six in ten—admitted to getting news from social media, particularly Facebook (Matsa & Lu, 2016). This is a potential problem because social media has no requirement to be neutral other than public perception. Of course, accused companies deny that any such violations happen and insist that if they did, it would be purely by accident or due to rogue employees.

Though difficult to prove either way, accusations against social media regarding neutrality violations happen periodically. For instance, Facebook has been accused of manipulating its "trending topics" headlines on several occasions. These accusations—which should be emphasized as being only accusations—have included such things as suppressing conservative news and adding topics to the list that weren't trending which caused them to become trending topics (Gunaratna, 2016). This is a major problem, considering a significant part of the population of planet Earth is on Facebook and sees those trending headlines. To Facebook's credit, it has taken actions to try to ensure the neutrality of its headlines.

Sometimes, the suggestions from sites are simply incorrect. Facebook's headlines have, from time to time, rotated fake news into the mix though the site now offers the option to report suspected fake headlines. Google Search, which is the main way of finding things online, shows what it hopes are quick answers to questions. Searching for an address, business hours, size conversions, and various other things turns up a card at the top of search results with an answer. These cards are also used to power answers from Google Home, Google's voice-controlled assistant, and Google Now, Google's phone assistant. The general expectation is that these cards are accurate. However, they're created automatically so that's not always the case, though Google manually fixes them if problems are reported. Even Google's algorithms occasionally fall for fake news articles or completely incorrect information. Usually, it means something like the hours the cards provide for a business aren't quite right. At times though, Google's instant answers have claimed such things as the Republican party being a group of Nazis, and Barack Obama planning a coup d'état (Murphy, 2017).

Though showing fake news and incorrect information is probably not intentional on the part of online services, many of these services do manipulate what they show to visitors. Page views are what allow ads to be shown, which is what brings in revenue. Many sites try to show you topics they think match your interests and views in order to keep you coming back and digging deeper. Google search results, Facebook news feeds, and other sites may provide something entirely different based on who you are. Even unintentionally, it's easy to get caught in a bubble that reflects what you think, whether those themes happen to be true or not. In this way, you already experience the worst of a non-neutral internet without even realizing it. There are ways to escape the bubble, but they require using alternate services and actively seeking out other perspectives, things interest tailoring makes increasingly difficult to do. On a non-neutral Internet, this becomes all but impossible because your ISP can make it more difficult to use those alternate services and to reach out of the bubble to explore more perspectives.

This begins to look like the Western Union of 1876. The issue of whether Facebook could manipulate an election has even been posed on multiple occasions. While the company denies that it has or ever would do that, it has manipulated users in other ways. In 2014, the world learned about a 2012 study where an academic journal worked with Facebook to study how removing all the negative or all the positive posts from user feeds would affect people's emotions. This study affected more than half a million people, without their consent or knowledge (Hill, 2014). If you don't have the option to leave because of your internet plan, there is no escape from a site manipulating your thoughts or emotions other than simply not using the Internet. Manipulating world affairs may not be difficult when 1.2 billion people or more spend a lot of their free time looking at your service or you control their information.

Large companies controlling large chunks of the Internet in this way has been justified by some with the claim that providing those services is a natural monopoly, a monopoly that develops due to a high cost of entry into an industry. The claim has been applied to Google in particular, citing the market share of the company (Yang, 2009). Those claims are somewhat problematic considering that none of the services Google provides are exclusive—all of them are offered by other just as accessible companies as well.

The easy access to news and information that the Internet provides should be empowering. However, curated headlines and limited access to information build a bubble that limits how informed people are able to be and has the possibility of affecting global affairs. ISPs have already been caught throttling services to discourage people from using them, and pushing their own services over others—which is especially problematic when it's their in-house news networks being prioritized. Ensuring that the Internet remains neutral, especially with fake news and incidents of incorrect information appearing on trustworthy sites, is incredibly important.

. . .

7 · Supporting Innovation

The Internet as it is today grew out of a neutral ecosystem; one where ISPs did not discriminate against any data on their networks. Increasing bandwidth usage forced ISPs to improve their networks to support more use, giving rise to more bandwidth and more online innovation with new services that couldn't exist without those better networks in place. High bandwidth services such as streaming video—Netflix, YouTube, and Hulu, for example—appeared and were able to grow in popularity based on the quality of their services rather than limitations imposed by ISPs. Some of these services compete with cable service, which is often provided by the same companies providing Internet service. In general, online innovation and customer demand has been a major driving factor in the evolution of ISP networks.

This is not to say that ISPs have no role in innovation. Without the support of ISPs, nothing in the online world would be able to deliver services to customers. Companies that provide Internet access need to continue to improve their networks to expand how much data they can carry as the Internet grows. Bandwidth requirements and data usage grow as services push more data and people use online services for more of their lives. Virtual reality, 4K video, and realtime streaming are all growing in use and require far more bandwidth. Without the support of ISPs, these types of new technologies will be less usable. The invention of bandwidth-heavy services could slow to a halt as networks struggle to meet their demands. Network expansions require investments from telecoms, which could be impacted by net neutrality regulations.

Opponents of net neutrality, including ISPs themselves, suggest that net neutrality regulations will change how ISPs invest in their networks, making them invest less in network improvements. According to ISP lobbying and advertising, net neutrality will be expensive because of the need to adhere to regulations. That, plus heavy-handed regulations on how ISPs can manage their networks and the traffic over them, could prevent network upgrades from happening in a timely manner. However, ISPs have explained to investors—then quickly backtracked after realizing investors weren't the only ones listening—that net neutrality would have little to no effect on their network investments.

A similar line of thought suggests that allowing ISPs to collect extra revenue by charging upstream services for bandwidth or prioritization would allow ISP network expansions to happen faster. The problem with this reasoning is that most ISPs are publicly-traded companies, meaning that there are others who have financial stakes in their success. This also takes the optimistic position that service providers would invest additional profits back into their networks at all. Companies that provide Internet service already have record-high profits and have been spending less on their networks already as a percentage of their revenue.

Charging more for bandwidth or for prioritization may allow for faster network improvements, but at the cost of innovation in upstream services. Fees that online services could need to pay to ISPs for delivering their content is funding that online services are unable to invest back into themselves. What this means for consumers is either higher costs for the same service, if online services choose to pass those costs onto their customers, or fewer improvements and fewer new features. A slowdown of improvements in the online space would also be driven by less competition as established companies could drone out startups by being prioritized better or by negotiating exclusivity agreements with ISPs. Due to the fact that ISPs are the only way a customer can access those services, ISPs could extort services for large amounts of money and it would be difficult for services to argue. If an online service can't be reached, the company can no longer make money so it would be forced to pay or risk being blocked. This looks similar to the telephone network in the 1970s, when running a network required paying AT&T for the use of their long distance lines, something far too expensive for small startups.

Service providers blocking apps to favor others is not unheard-of on the modern Internet. ISPs, especially mobile carriers, have a history of restricting and throttling specific services on their networks. Comcast and Netflix, for example, have a rocky past with throttling of Netflix's streaming. Netflix agreed to pay Comcast for better speeds after many of its customers cancelled subscriptions because the service wasn't usable on Comcast connections. In 2012, a major carrier began blocking or slowing down Apple's FaceTime video chat. The company argued that customers needed to subscribe to a more expensive text and voice plan in order to access the service (Shein, 2012). The carrier eventually relented due to public outcry, but still restricted customers on unlimited data plans from using FaceTime.

Prioritizing an ISP-friendly internet over a more consumer and business friendly internet could be a poor choice for the economy because most companies are not ISPs. The U.S. is the home of many of the original large online services. Google, Yahoo, Netflix, EBay, and nearly any other online name you can think of that has been around for a long time likely started in the U.S. and likely still calls the U.S. home. It's easy to take for granted the effect those companies have on the global economy. Data given to these companies—and there is a lot of it, from photos, to shopping preferences, to interest information never explicitly given to them— is on U.S. soil and governed by local regulations.

If the online ecosystem changes, so could the preferred country of Silicon Valley. U.S. companies themselves could choose to relocate overseas and already have infrastructure in place to operate in other countries. In some cases, international alternatives to U.S. companies exist. Alternatives to Google, for example, exist in Russia as Yandex and in China as Baidu, and there is little preventing other companies from springing up. Arguably, with education systems in other countries doing more to teach technical proficiency, skills might better be found abroad and a non neutral internet could be a push to make other countries more appealing.

Parallels can be drawn between the world of online innovation and the U.S. manufacturing sector. In the U.S., the manufacturing sector has suffered from cultural changes, education issues, and in some places, policies. Due to that, manufacturing has largely moved out of the United States to countries such as China where the climate is much better. Something similar could happen to the Internet if policies turn more favorable elsewhere. While China's restricted internet may seem an unlikely place for online innovation as seen in the U.S., they have their own innovative online services. There are also other countries waiting. India and Mongolia have expanding technology sectors with their own developing technology hubs. These countries are primed to take the place of the U.S. as a leader in online innovation. Stories of "The Next Silicon Valley" have never come to fruition, but in a country where starting the next big thing is too expensive and too difficult because of a non neutral internet, that could change.

A divided and throttled Internet also has the potential to harm offline innovation. The Internet has, for better or worse, created the assumption that the next big thing will be yet another online service full of the latest buzzwords. That doesn't need to be the case. The next big thing could instead be an invention built in someone's garage in their spare time. Reference materials that may be needed to develop it are likely more readily available and up to date online than they are at a local library. Online sources such as Wikipedia provide information that can be updated as fast as minutes after announcements of new data. Others, such as StackOverflow, provide quick access to other people's knowledge in a question and answer format.

Research has shown that adults who have reliable access to the Internet are more likely to try to learn more about the world. Of the people in the study, 10-30% more had done some form of personal learning (depending on the Internet devices they had access to) than those who did not have a broadband Internet connection (Horrigan, 2016). Of the personal learners, more than half reported they did some of their learning online. This underscores the need for access to a wide variety of viewpoints online. ISPs manipulating what users have access to becomes dangerous when it comes to making sure people are informed and are able to continue to learn. Encouraging such learning helps support innovation, online and off.

The effects of a non neutral internet aren't fully known. Net neutrality will have an effect on online innovation in some form—though not necessarily bad. A two-tier internet may find itself with only business or high priority services in the fast lane, versus a mix of consumer services in both places. The guarantee of a reliable, faster tier could spur innovation in ways not yet imagined (Nordrum, 2017). There are a lot of unknowns. No ISP has provided restricted access to the Internet on a wide enough scale to make good predictions. However, the differences in learning driven by Internet access and the risk of shutting out new online services make allowing ISPs to be a driving factor for innovation a potentially dangerous proposition.

. . .

8 · Privacy as a Commodity

It doesn't take much to track an individual online. Seemingly small details like a phone number or email address can be used to tie pieces of information together from various places. Online subscriptions can reveal interests and shopping habits, as well as online affiliations. Who an individual talks to, texts, or calls can indicate the type of people they affiliate themselves with and life affairs like legal involvements. Services comb through this information to build a picture of who a person is and what their interests are to better target advertisements to them. Even seemingly innocuous details like a particular pattern of purchases can reveal all sorts of information—including things like unannounced pregnancies.

Almost everything online has some form of tracking installed. Google Analytics, a widely used tracking service, makes it possible for website owners to drill down into all kinds of information about visitors.

Advertisers gather data about visitors that they sell or use directly to target advertisements to the people who seem most likely to click on them. That sort of data is extremely valuable on a wide scale—the U.S. was worth over $2.8 billion in advertising revenue to Facebook in a single quarter in 2015 (Gibbs, 2016). What's worse, is that this tracking isn't limited to a single site—visiting any website with Facebook "like" buttons is enough for Facebook to track where you've been—and there are many other services that do the same thing. This is often not a known problem for the layperson, but it can become one when a quick search results in a month of banner ads for something embarrassing (or amusing to the people sitting nearby on public transit). Fortunately, there are relatively easy ways to prevent this sort of tracking—browser add-ons such as ublock or Ghostery that block most tracking services.

Online tracking is extremely pervasive. In 2014, Facebook and MasterCard were in the news for a new data sharing agreement, something that could mean the two companies could connect your Facebook information and your card transactions if you were part of Facebook's Asia Pacific data (Head, 2014). Even the government has gotten caught in data sharing agreements for data otherwise assumed to be confidential. In January 2015, Healthcare.gov, the federal health insurance exchange, was caught collecting private health information and forwarding it on to third party tracking services (Christian, 2015). The Internet of Things makes online tracking even worse. Devices and the backing services that make them smart build databases of when people are not home and what things they buy in order to make life easier.

Tracking isn't limited to online services. ISPs can also track their users and have access to a lot of information about them. While using secure sites helps, it's still possible to see what websites are visited and how often. Hiding this usually requires buying access to a VPN service which hides traffic from your internet provider or by using a technology like Tor. At some point, though, the company or service you access the web through needs to know where to send traffic. Smartphones, Internet of Things devices, and other devices that use the Internet need to reach out online to fetch updates and other information; seeing what they talk to makes it possible to figure out at a minimum what company made them.

Service providers engaging in tracking practices is not just theoretical. Two ISPs were forced to admit in 2015 to using "supercookies," bits of tracking information on a phone or computer, that tracked people even when they weren't on the two companies' networks. Information gathered this way was not gathered with customer consent or knowledge (Christian, 2015). Supercookies allow companies using them to track much of an individual's online activity without getting noticed.

Even cell phones, convenient as they are, provide a wealth of tracking information to online services and ISPs. Since most people carry their phone everywhere, it's possible to track a person's habits and gather information about their interests based on where they go. This is how Google Now manages to figure out where your home and your work are, without you actually telling it. This is also why, days after a restaurant visit, Google Maps may ask you for a review of the place you ate at. There have even been cases of governments tracking activists based on their cell phones (Goodin, 2014), though none confirmed yet in the U.S.

Information gathered from tracking, online or off, can have real-world consequences. Tracking information can be used to determine all sorts of things about a person's political views, income, health, and even when they're most likely to be home. Should this leak—either through hacking or to the highest bidder—it opens up a lot of potential problems. It makes it possible to trick people into giving their information to the wrong website (phishing) and even opens up burglary possibilities. Sometimes, revealing information is intentional. Target, which uses targeted advertisements and coupons mailed to people's houses based on their purchases, has enough statistical information to predict what's happening in a person's life. In widely reported case of accidentally revealing private information, Target announced the pregnancy of a teenager to her family by mailing her targeted coupons before she had a chance to tell her family herself (Christian, 2015).

Making privacy a commodity introduces another split

between the informed elite who can pay for access to both information and privacy, and those who can't. Already, there are problems with accessing the Internet in the U.S., with price being the main reason people don't have a connection. What's worse still, is that being able to afford privacy does not make privacy accessible. Using a VPN or Tor requires some technical knowledge that doesn't come easily to everyone. As the Internet becomes more accessible, more people are opened to the perils of their data being sold to the highest bidder or hacked, simply due to not knowing that protection is needed. The fight for equality needs to extend beyond the physical world and into the digital one, especially as the two mingle. ISPs appear to want to be the ones to take away that equality because charging extra for privacy or simply selling collected data adds to their bottom line.

Disturbingly, some companies have claimed that poor people simply don't want privacy. In early 2017, a civil rights group funded by Comcast argued that people living in poverty would rather have ads than privacy protections (Fang, 2017). The group went on to say that this is due to the fact that ads lower the cost of accessing the Internet, which is the same as arguing that commercials lower the cost of cable TV. While ads do provide additional revenue, the impact they have on the cost of consumer service is negligible.

Companies have even made the claim that too small of a percentage of their users have configured anti-tracking to indicate that people actually care about online privacy. However, these companies have so many users that a small percentage—which includes only the people who know how to change those settings—is millions of users. Five percent of Firefox users enabled DoNotTrack (it's now turned on by default) in their browser in 2015. The percentage is small, but amounts to between 25 and 50 million people (Christian, 2015).

The data that ISPs are able to gather is massive and concerning given that even the most innocent and innocuous information can be sold for targeted services. It's worth recalling that the United States constitution guarantees freedom of speech and freedom of the press, which is part of the protection from government overreach. When making arguments such as that, ISPs are arguing not only that people in poverty don't deserve privacy, but that as corporations they are allowed to take away that privacy.

From a technological standpoint, there is little reason for an internet provider to keep records of what its customers do online, especially not for an extended period. There are valid reasons to inspect traffic in the shorter term and complete forbidding ISPs from doing so would be bad for the health and safety of the Internet. Keeping a network free of malware and protecting against illegal activity and hacking attempts is important. ISPs would not be and are not restricted from doing that. However, maintaining long term records of that traffic has little technical use other than tracking individuals. Indeed, some ISPs, such as Sonic.net in northern California, already have privacy policies that prevent them from storing information about the habits of users long term. Sonic.net keeps user data for only two weeks. This isn't the shortest period to keep user data—there are VPN services that do not keep logs at all—but it is among the shortest among major ISPs, who keep data up to 18 months (Greenberg, 2012).

Extending the collection of user habits into selling said data is, of course, a profit-driven activity. Many online services sell or share data, in some form or another, in order to provide a free service. Internet access is neither free nor provided by an industry that suffers from low profit margins. Selling such data, even indirectly for the purpose of selling targeted ads to be shown on web pages, is not required to keep the telecom industry afloat. As it would be a way to increase profits, it's hard to fight against an ISP that wanted to do that and there isn't any escape should yours decide to.

Part of an ideal neutral Internet is transparency regulations. Transparency about how personal information is used is closely regulated in certain industries, such as banking where breakdowns of how data is used and how its use can be limited are provided periodically. ISPs are not held to anything resembling that sort of regulations when it comes to information about what you do online. In 2017, Congress voted to allow Internet providers to sell information about their users, even though most would assume their service provider isn't sharing what they do online. If ISPs are required to disclose details of what they're tracking and sharing in terms of how you use the Internet, that itself is a deterrent from tracking and sharing in the first place.

. . .

UNDERMINING NEUTRALITY

9 · Internet Monopolies

In the United States, most people have access to only one or two internet service providers at home. Only 28% had access to three or more ISPs for speeds one might consider tolerable, and 9% for speeds one might consider "fast" as of 2014 (Helper, 2014). This means that at home if you have a problem with your Internet provider as a company—be it that you disagree with its views, you can't deal with customer support when a problem comes up, you don't trust the company, or you simply can't afford to pay for its service, there is no escape. Access to the Internet is not a luxury anymore, so the possibility of simply not doing business with your ISP isn't an option.

Since that data was collected, there have been acquisitions and mergers in the ISP industry. There are likely some who have seen the number of ISP options at home fall, especially with the Charter and Time Warner Cable deal. Others may not have seen their options change, but the ones they have may now be larger companies that are more difficult to deal with and that care less about the local communities they serve. Mergers and acquisitions in the ISP world are common. Originally, Internet access was provided by a far greater number of companies that eventually merged and were acquired by others, leaving the big household names that are familiar today. Acquisitions can be a healthy part of a business growing, but in the ISP business have gotten somewhat out of hand, starting the effect of centralizing control over access to the Internet.

These mergers have sometimes been approved by the FCC with certain conditions intended to protect customers and competition. However, conditions imposed for an approval are not always well enforced or have been easy for ISPs to work around. One such case was in 2016, when Charter acquired Time Warner Cable and BrightHouse to become Spectrum. The FCC required Spectrum to bring broadband of a minimum speed to 1 million homes and businesses in an area with a competitor, something called overbuilding. Charter was able to make an agreement with the FCC that the company could buy other ISPs and count that towards its competition agreements (Brodkin, 2016c).

The state of mobile data is marginally better. Most people have access to more than three providers for standard mobile data speeds (Helper, 2014). While this looks promising, the mobile data market isn't as diverse as it appears. While there are many MVNOs (mobile virtual network operators) who you can buy service through, all of them piggyback on the networks of four major U.S. networks: Verizon, T-Mobile, AT&T, and Sprint. It's difficult not to because the infrastructure investments required to build a mobile network with reasonable coverage are huge, and the large networks are willing to sell capacity. It's unlikely a new contender would be able to get a foothold when they would need the funding to build nationwide wireless infrastructure. Further, mobile data is not something that can replace a home Internet connection because mobile data is far slower, with substantially lower data caps, making the more competitive mobile business somewhat of a moot point when discussing wired ISPs.

The mobile data market is also suffering from acquisitions and mergers. T-Mobile and Sprint are reportedly considering a merger which would bring the four major networks down to three (Fung, 2017a). The size of the largest carriers, is large enough to rival that of Bell prior to its breakup in the 1980s and by some accounts is larger. With recent acquisitions of DirecTV by AT&T and Yahoo by Verizon, large ISPs continue to grow not only in the Internet space, but the content creation space. Competition that does exist appears to be ready to shrink, if the FCC were to approve additional mergers or acquisitions, while providers pick up ownership of more media outlets.

The lack of options is unfortunate but not surprising. Unlike most other industries, building an internet service provider is prohibitively difficult. It requires large, expensive installations of equipment, and requires buying Internet service (to resell) from an existing service provider which could become a competitor. The initial costs are so high that a new service provider is unlikely to make a profit for several years after construction (Brodkin, 2014a). Of course, it isn't impossible to create a new ISP, but it is far too difficult and too expensive for most people and even companies. Even Google is getting out of the fiber business after entering a few cities. Consider how difficult it would be to start a new electric company, ignoring regulatory problems, without using the existing transmission lines; starting a new ISP is similar.

Competition and room for small ISPs is limited from the start in new neighborhoods, because construction usually only accounts for one provider. It's wholly possible to install lines for multiple ISPs, but it's rare for that to actually be done. Exclusivity agreements from existing ISPs sometimes are made by lobbying the locality which may even make it a breach of contract to support more than one provider (Szoka, Starr, & Henke, 2013). Unfortunately, new construction is where it would be least expensive to allow for competition because the digging is where the majority of installation costs are.

Apartment complexes tend to be even worse, supporting a particular provider exclusively for a service. There's even less of an escape in that case because even if a different provider has infrastructure nearby, contractual agreements between the landlord and provider, or construction requirements can make connecting impossible. It's worth noting, however, that landlords can sometimes negotiate better pricing for tenants. In general, that is not the case. Regardless, the lack of competition allows the provider a lot of room for overcharging and offering poor service since there's no other option to turn to.

The problems with existing infrastructure are that it's difficult to share and there's no enforced requirement for its owners to do so. A particular ISP may be the only provider available to a neighborhood simply because the lines there belong to that ISP. That makes sense, but gives the ISP a monopoly on the service. The ISP wouldn't share its infrastructure because it would then be allowing competition to eat into its market. It is possible to run lines over public infrastructure such as telephone poles depending on the area, but doing so for a new company is expensive and comes with no guarantee of customers.

Infrastructure is not the only factor limiting telecom competition. A conspiracy theory of telecom backroom deals has existed for a long time, likely because it's exciting, of telecom executives dividing up territory and chuckling about profits. The reality is less colorful. Infrastructure limitations—real or artificially imposed—are the main driver of limited options. However, the imagined backroom deal is not entirely inaccurate, as more ISP practices have come to light. In 2017, Charter and Comcast agreed not to compete in their new wireless businesses after buying parts of the wireless spectrum to build networks (Bode, 2017). Charter even admitted that it avoided competing with other cable companies in order to leave the option of buying them on the table (Brodkin, 2016c) while getting FCC approval for becoming Spectrum. Charter's CEO explained,

"When I talked to the FCC, I said I can't overbuild another cable company, because then I could never buy it, because you always block those. It's really about overbuilding telephone companies." (Brodkin, 2016c)

Charter's CEO went on to explain that competing with phone companies was easier than competing with other cable companies. His theory was that it was easier to win over customers from phone companies, which often have slower infrastructure. That also is likely what makes buying a phone company less appealing to a cable company such as Charter, which is why they would be willing to forgo the possibility of acquiring one.

This type of avoidance of competing and agreements not to compete are extremely anti-consumer. Without competition, ISPs have no incentive to improve their services while keeping prices low. There is no option to turn to if prices go up or quality of service goes down. Even worse, there is no escape if ISPs use a non neutral Internet to curate what their customers see.

Internet service providers have even blocked and limited taxpayer funded networks. In 2008, Comcast sued the city of Chattanooga, Tennessee to block the city from building its own local ISP (Comcast Sues EPB, 2008). Municipal networks, discussed in more depth later, tend to be better for their community when implemented properly—but large ISPs prefer to fight them as they would lose sections of their regional monopolies. What's perhaps most upsetting about this is that in some cases, taxpayers have already paid for those networks but local governments are not allowed to provide access to them. Telecom lobbying has limited the Chattanooga municipal broadband project to serving the area it was originally built in, even though it could provide access to surrounding communities. Most offensively, the first 100Gbps network in the U.S. was built in Washington, D.C. in 2006, but telecoms have successfully gotten its use restricted to local nonprofits —even though it is one of the fastest networks in the country (Connolly, 2014).

When service providers are forced to compete, their prices often drop substantially. When Google Fiber announced it would offer Internet service in Tennessee, for example, ISPs in the overlapping service areas suddenly began offering substantially lower prices and more products. One of them cut prices for some products by as much as 40% (McGee, 2015). In Charlotte, another made its plans six times faster when Google Fiber was expected to become available (Brodkin, 2015a).

Unfortunately, the supposed savior of provider choice, Google Fiber, is no longer expanding its network. Other local (not municipal) ISPs, such as Greenlight in Rochester, New York exist, but not on a large enough scale to compete with a company the size of most large ISPs. Indeed, while Greenlight is the preferred ISP in Rochester, the company's coverage map is small. Larger ISPs appear not to have bothered to take much notice of the new competitor, offering the same service plans and prices as always, other than changes rolled out as part of acquisitions.

The fact that large telecoms are willing to ignore new competition highlights the need for more competition. Other ISP options are in some cases so large that they don't need to care—at least not yet—about the newcomer in Rochester. Driving customers away is not something that concerns them yet because even if Greenlight continues to grow, they have the upper hand in dealing with the newcomer. Big-name ISPs can afford to drop prices and offer plans that undercut Greenlight, while Greenlight has needed to expand slowly based on customer interest because of a much smaller bottom line.

The other side of the monopoly is online services. Companies have realized that they can convince users to join and never leave their ecosystems. Google Home, Amazon Alexa, and similar products make life easier, but also—as they improve—become a permanent tool. Switching from one to the other is possible, but they don't offer the same features. Other things, like iCloud or Google Chromecast, tie into a lot of devices, but are normally fairly exclusive to the company that owns them. Moving away from iCloud to Google Photos is not an easy task, for example. Moving from Chromecast to Apple TV or the reverse is potentially worse because there are devices specific to one or the other and buying a new collection of devices might be needed. If your ISP prefers to encourage one ecosystem over another, that's even worse because migrating may not be something that's up to you.

In either case, choices are limited. ISPs can limit access to some information and encourage other information and sometimes offer exclusive services. Online services want to keep control of your data so they can learn about you. There are no requirements for being open to other ecosystems. Until there is competition, providers can offer any prices or walled gardens they want because there is no alternative or cheaper option. With how quickly ISPs are able to offer lower prices and provide better service when a competitor arrives, it's clear that it's possible to do better while maintaining their bottom lines. Unfortunately, there's no competitive push for improvements because competition is so rare and where it does exist, appears to be closely controlled.

. . .

10 · Data Caps

One of the ways ISPs—particularly mobile data providers—use their ability to charge what they want is with data caps. Data caps are wildly unpopular with ISP customers, with their introduction usually sparking news articles and customer complaints. Data Caps (also called Bandwidth Caps and sometimes shortened to "caps") are a limit on how much you can upload and download through your internet provider, typically on a monthly basis. Usage Based Pricing (UBP) is related—rather than capping data, you're charged for how much or how little you use.

Most people are familiar with data caps and UBP from cell phone data plans, although data caps on home service also exist. Usually, they're sold as a quality and fairness measure, so that no one person can hog the service provider's network. Whether that's widely believed is questionable, since customer protest usually causes ISPs to roll out data caps as a way to voluntarily reduce bills or as "tests" in a certain area. It turns out that, by the admission of ISPs themselves, data caps and UBP have little to nothing to do with usage. Instead, caps are more profit driven and tend to influence customers to spend more for their Internet than they need to.

It is true that bandwidth is a limited commodity on networks. There is only so much data that can pass through a network at the same time, limited by the technologies in use and the laws of physics. Mobile networks have some of the most limited bandwidth because they operate differently than wired networks. There is only so much "spectrum" as it's called to go around and their range is limited based on signal strength, weather, and other factors. Wired networks have limitations also, but are generally much more capable than wireless networks with current technology.

To their credit, although data caps aren't put in place for limiting network usage, they are actually effective at doing so. Generally, people who are accustomed to capped plans are good at keeping track of how much data they use and managing it over the course of a month, and use less towards the beginning of the month. Towards the end of the month, they'll use more in order to get all the data they feel they're paying for. This isn't terribly surprising since intuitively most people want to make sure they're not spending more data than they have, but then don't want to "lose" the rest of it (Fung, 2015).

Internet service providers have admitted that data caps have nothing to do with network capacity (Masnick, 2013). In some cases, ISPs have dropped the capacity and fairness claim altogether and have asked their customer support representatives to stop using that explanation when customers ask (Epstein, Mills, Smith, & Wehner, 2015). Not only that, but ISPs have told the government that network congestion is not a problem in a survey of wireless and wired ISPs (Brodkin, 2014b).

Indeed, if their own admissions aren't enough, mobile carriers have been moving more of their services and pushing more customers to their supposedly congested data networks. Some carriers route certain phone calls over their LTE data networks using what's called Voice over LTE (VoLTE) (Lewis, 2014) which can provide better call quality. One carrier has even been accused of forcing customers to switch to wireless from landlines, at times without customer knowledge by forbidding employees from repairing copper phone lines. While voice calls don't necessarily use the data network, the availability of VoLTE on some networks makes it a very real possibility that they are. "Unlimited" data plans from all four major networks are also making a comeback in the latest fight to offer the most desirable plans to potential customers in the latest curiosity in the claims of limited bandwidth.

As high-bandwidth services like Netflix, Skype, and other streaming services are adopted by more people, more network capacity is required. However, the amount of data that is zero-rated—that is, it can be transferred without using up a data cap—makes it clear that capacity is not currently a huge concern. AT&T for example rolled out streaming services for live TV a la DirecTV quickly and without capacity problems (though not without other problems). Verizon ran a series of ads in 2017 touting data-free streaming of NFL games on its network.

T-Mobile, which describes itself as "The Uncarrier," offered similar zero-rated data services. One of the company's former plans, called Binge On, offered free streaming from a variety of services without counting against data limits. Even bandwidth-heavy services like Netflix were available under the plan, though limited to lower quality video. T-Mobile allowed any video streaming service to join the Binge On program assuming they met a series of technical requirements.

Verizon is even reportedly considering stopping laying fiber optic lines, which can involve expensive construction, in favor of other technologies with testing in spring 2017. The ISP seems to expect that 5G networks, which it has referred to as "wireless fiber" (Weissberger, 2016), are a fast-enough replacement. Using wireless allows for fast expansions of network segments at a low cost so capacity can be expanded with minimal expense or disruption to customers because there is no extensive digging and installation. Variants of 5G are, in theory, the next mobile data technology after 4G/LTE. If 5G is actually capable of what the company hopes it will be, then wireless network capacity should grow far beyond its current capabilities, making data caps even harder to defend. While 5G won't be used immediately to extend existing networks over long distances, it may be used as a last-mile connection to customer houses for TV and Internet service.

If network congestion is not a problem, then perhaps it's the cost of moving data that's the problem. However, bandwidth costs for ISPs are far lower than the majority of consumers could ever hope to see on their own plans. This is what makes high-bandwidth services like Netflix or YouTube possible—they too pay for the data they send to you. Sending a gigabyte of data across the Internet costs less than a penny and in some cases, may even be free depending on the agreements between backbone providers (Jameson, 2016). According to the Government Accountability Office, ISPs report that even heavy users—those who use far more than the average household per month in data—don't actually cost substantially more to deliver Internet to (Brodkin, 2014b). At those rates, using the average overage fee per gigabyte that most customers see, the overage fees are more than a 2000% markup in price.

The usual defense of data caps provided when these costs are mentioned is the fact that building and maintaining networks is expensive. That would provide a reason for why the per-gigabyte cost of moving data across the Internet as a customer is so high, while the cost for an ISP to move data is so low. Such a suggestion is problematic when considering that ISPs have been spending less on networks as a percentage of revenue while seeing average revenue per user skyrocket (Fung, 2014). Part of the reason for lower spending on networks is that many ISPs offer service over the same networks they installed years prior, though with various upgrades in place (Anderson, 2012). The same 2014 study concludes that the explanations for data caps given by ISPs are not entirely true, and are intended to disguise the fact that they are making record profits—while complaining about ongoing revenue problems.

Unsurprisingly with how much overage data costs, data caps make Internet access more expensive. People are so afraid of going over their caps and getting charged overage fees (or having access cut off entirely) that they often buy more expensive plans than they need for higher caps. Few people are fully aware of how much data they use over the course of a month on their home Internet, so when data caps are introduced, they pay more for data they don't need. What's more, is that people on plans that did not limit data paid almost 80% less per gigabyte of data, which is a huge difference (Fung, 2015). That statistic alone shows that claims that metered (limited) plans are less expensive are not telling the whole story. Capped plans may be less expensive in terms of base cost, but because users tend to pay for more than they need or for expensive overages, the lower prices are deceptive.

In theory, usage based pricing is a more fair evolution of the cap. Rather than stopping access after the cap is reached or charging overages, you pay for data as you use it. This is the way ISPs pay for data from the backbone providers they pay for a connection to the wider Internet, aside from any special agreements. Regulating ISPs as utilities could lend itself more towards UBP than flat monthly fees for service. In an ideal world, this could be a good answer to some anti net neutrality practices ISPs engage in.

In practice, UBP suffers the same problems as data caps and tends to be paired with data caps, meaning customers get the worst of both worlds. Not only are you paying for data as you use it, you pay overages if you use too much. Logically, this doesn't make a lot of sense either because if you're paying for the data you move, you would expect the cost of using more would already be built into the price. Paying more for data during peak hours—as utility companies often have you do for electricity—might make sense. Implemented in either way, UBP comes with the problem that it can discourage the use of high-bandwidth services like Netflix or streaming news.

The biggest problems with data caps and UBP is that they are not applied equally so they limit choices. ISPs exempt certain services from counting as data used, or zero-rate, which gives an incentive to use some services over others—a problem when your ISP owns the news network it zero-rates. Caps also force customers to choose what they do online carefully, or risk incurring overages or running out of data. This means that users who require data for different things—working from home, for example—are less able to make use of other services. The choice is a problem because the Internet is widely used for staying informed and for looking up reference material for work. If nothing else, limiting choices can also limit competition, as it's difficult to start another streaming service or news network when accessing it is too expensive for people with limited data. Caps don't provide the fairness that ISPs once claimed. They're more expensive and less fair to everyone, though they do provide the catharsis of thinking your neighbor's Netflix use will be kept in check before it affects you.

Using the utility analogy again, the problem with UBP in particular is how easy—and potentially profitable—it is to apply pricing unevenly. Utility companies have no way of knowing what the electricity they're providing is being used for. There is no way, barring Internet of Things devices that might report more information back to the utility, for them to know if they're powering a toaster or a TV. The Internet is different because ISPs are able to see what websites they're sending data to because they need to know where to send traffic. UBP needs strong regulations to ensure ISPs are neither allowed to care about your data nor are they allowed to price different data differently.

Looking into the future, data caps have another

problem: they can influence network planning. Due to the fact that data caps do have the side effect of lowering bandwidth usage, ISPs may plan network expansions around the lower data usage, which might push off certain network improvements. This further entrenches data caps because ISP networks may not be able to handle the flood of data should ISPs uncap their plans. An ISP that plans around artificially lower data needs would need to implement more network changes in a shorter period to uncap its customers. Those network upgrades could have otherwise been spread out over time along with the costs.

All in all, data caps are an expensive and generally unfair limit on data usage. When applied the same across the entire Internet, they are less of a problem and do actually limit bandwidth usage, as ISPs claim. This can help in developing networks, especially in underserved areas where alternative network technologies may be needed. However, caps don't appear to be necessary to keep developed networks running smoothly based on ISP admissions. Data caps should require a technical justification, not just one from an ISP's public relations department.

. . .

11 · Free Data

The practice of zero-rating, which has gone mainstream fairly recently in the ISP world, is when certain online services don't count against a data cap. Depending on your provider, anything from NFL games to Pokémon Go might be free to use without using up your data. There are two ways carriers do this: by having the company behind the zero-rated service pay for the data use, or by simply not counting it for promotional reasons. For users, it seems pretty good because it looks like free data. Unfortunately, zero-rating brings a number of serious problems that hurt users in the longer term. It hurts competition between online services, limits and disincentives users from freely accessing the Internet, and costs more.

The idea of zero-rating only makes sense in the context of limited Internet plans. On a (mostly standard) home Internet plan that doesn't have a cap, zero-rating has no purpose—there is no limit to exempt online activities from. If zero-rating is part of the perks of a data plan (home or wireless), that likely indicates the plan has a data cap that could put you at risk of overages. A plan with a flat rate and no zero-rating is better overall because it doesn't come with the pressure to buy more data than you need and doesn't come with the effects of a closed ecosystem.

What's nefarious about zero-rating is how hard it is to get past the "free stuff" part of it. The problem with free data is that it is getting paid for even if you aren't the one paying for it—and you may be paying for it in ways you don't realize. Carriers and service providers still want the data paid for so if you're not paying for it, then the service you're using data-free likely is. That service, in turn, cares about its bottom line as well and may add or increase its own subscription fees. In that case, you are paying for the data you're using—the charges just aren't part of your Internet bill. If you have a data plan that allows you to stream sports for free, the sports network you're streaming from may need to pay for the data you're using. Users can end up paying more—first for the data subscription package with zero-rating, and again for the data they're (invisibly) paying for via the subscription fees for the zero-rated service. Service providers explain that they don't "double-dip", which is likely true, but that doesn't mean it isn't a good deal for them (Sottek, 2016).

Zero-rating can cost more in other ways as well. If a service doesn't count against data limits, it can be hard to say no to using it. However, that can push using a paid service over a free one—which again, means you're paying for your data and possibly more than you would need to otherwise. If you choose to use the subscription-based service over a free one, then you may even be costing yourself more money in the long run.

The problems with zero-rating go deeper than customer bills. The practice can even be described as anti-competitive because it gives large advantages to the services that zero-rate their own apps. Zero-rating encourages the use of some services over others, even if the services that are being encouraged are biased, poor quality, or insecure. This can be particularly problematic when service providers zero-rate their in-house services. Zero-rating a service, even for a short time, has been shown to cause huge spikes in the usage of that service (Feamster, 2016). That means that where services are zero-rated, people are more likely to use the zero-rated services over alternatives. It's understandable because data plans tend to be expensive. Unfortunately, that makes it much more difficult for competition to grow, so there's little reason for the zero-rated services to offer better prices (or service). A new competitor would need to make the case for why someone should use their limited data on it, versus using another service that doesn't count towards their data. In the end, the user loses to potentially worse service and higher prices.

ISPs already zero-rate the services they own over alternatives. Verizon, in 2016, announced that some of its own online services would not count towards customer data. In particular this applied to Go90, the ISP's in-house video streaming service, which is free with ads. YouTube, Netflix, and other streaming services, which could be seen as competitors to Go90, would still count towards customer data limits (Brodkin, 2016a). AT&T does the same thing with DirecTV, allowing DirecTV subscribers to stream DirecTV without it counting against their data caps (Sottek, 2016).

A letter retrieved from the FCC website sent to AT&T in 2016 outlined just how anti-competitive zero-rating can be. In that letter the FCC explains, which it notes is a conservative estimate, how expensive it is zero-rate a service on AT&T's network. If you were to make a service zero-rated using the carrier's "Sponsored Data" arrangement, you could pay substantially more per customer who uses your service than a DirecTV subscription costs. Of course, AT&T owns DirecTV, so for AT&T, zero-rating DirecTV only costs network bandwidth. As a competitor to AT&T, you would be at a severe disadvantage when trying to sell your own video service to someone who uses DirecTV with AT&T.

"Using the reference example from your white paper stating that your Sponsored Data rates are similar to the discounted wholesale rates paid by major wireless resellers, we estimate for purposes of illustrating our concerns that an unaffiliated mobile video service provider would have to pay AT&T $16 a month to offer zero-rated service to a customer who uses just

10 minutes of LTE video per day, increasing to $47 for a customer using 30 minutes per day. These costs alone would represent 46 percent to 134 percent of DIRECTV Now's $35 retail price, against which third parties will be competing for AT&T Mobility customers, and would be borne in addition to all other costs of providing service by the unaffiliated provider. As consumers increasingly use mobile video services - a process which the practice of zero-rating mobile video usage will accelerate - these Sponsored Data charges could reasonably be expected to increase even more. By contrast, AT&T incurs no comparable cost to offer its own DIRECTV Now service on a zero-rated basis. If we understand these facts correctly, AT&T seems to present the unaffiliated provider with a choice that is unreasonable on its face: either pay a Sponsored Data rate (resulting in a $16-$47 per month - or higher - incremental cash cost not incurred by AT&T) that would make it very difficult, if not infeasible, to offer a competitively-priced service, or instead require its customers to pay significant amounts for their own usage of data while AT&T's zero-rated DIRECTV Now service offers customers the same usage for free."

Comcast has also attempted to offer zero-rated services, but went a little farther to avoid net neutrality outcry. The ISP introduced a streaming service in 2008, a few years after beginning a rollout of data caps on its network. ISPs running their own streaming services isn't rare and isn't problematic in and of itself. However, Comcast announced that its streaming service, which ran on Xbox, would be exempt from its data caps in order to provide an incentive for customers to use the service versus competing ones. This practice is a clear violation of net neutrality but the ISP argued that it wasn't. The streaming service did not operate over the open Internet—it was only on the ISP's network. So, the company argued, it was not a violation of net neutrality. After outcry, data caps were removed altogether, but the company continues to argue that it did not violate neutrality because the data only traveled through its own network and nowhere else.

By limiting competition like that, ISPs are also limiting your ability to choose what you use. The decision to stream an alternate news network that isn't zero-rated at the expense of giving up Netflix or working from home is a choice you could be forced to make. This contributes to your ISP creating a walled garden or closed ecosystem. You're artificially limited to only a portion of the Internet. There isn't necessarily an end to this—you might not be limited only to a particular streaming service, but to certain banking, insurance, and news networks, depending on how your ISP sets up its plan. At best, it can limit how wide of a world view you can see because you could be forced to use your ISP's news network instead of being able to compare several.

Any sort of zero-rating is unlikely to be uniform across different ISPs, contributing to different access to the Internet depending on where you are and what plans you pay for. Given the different zero-rating plans offered now or in the past, from T-Mobile Binge On to Verizon's Go90, different providers treat traffic in different ways. It's also subject to change, which can be problematic for an ISP you can't easily switch from. Changing business agreements and licensing fees could change what services don't use up data, including offerings from your ISP itself.

This becomes a much larger issue if you find yourself moving or otherwise changing ISPs. Due to differences in what services are zero-rated, you could find yourself canceling some subscriptions and creating new ones. This in itself can be a pain, but it doesn't stop there. You could end up needing to spend time moving over preferences to new services, when old ones already know about you. With regard to certain things like email service—which is already a problem if you use your ISP's email—moving can be a huge production because you need to tell everything you use that you have a new email address.

Zero-rating is regarded as such a problem that services which focus around it have been banned in several countries. India banned Facebook Free Basics, a non-neutral ISP based on zero-rating, in 2016. In 2017, Canada reaffirmed its opposition to zero-rating with a court battle that struck down unlimited streaming from a carrier called Quebecor (Summers, 2017). Even in the U.S., the FCC under Tom Wheeler took notice of zero-rating practices, regarding them with some suspicion such as with the letter to AT&T. The practice of allowing certain services to be exempt from data caps discourages competition and choice, creating a tiered Internet with privileges depending on how much data—or overages—you can afford. This can lead to a tiered or fast-laned Internet, depending on the ISP and its implementation —a free and slow "free" tier, and an unlimited, faster upper tier.

. . .

12 · Fast Lanes

From the net neutrality standpoint, tiered service does not refer to the different speed packages available currently. While these are sometimes referred to as speed tiers, those are allowed under net neutrality. On a neutral internet, Tiers from the net neutrality context refer to traffic or content tiers, in which different types of traffic or content are available differently depending on the plan. The distinction is that speed packages ISPs currently offer are applied equally across everything online. Meanwhile, in a tiered Internet you may find some services are available much faster than certain others. As a customer, you may find yourself choosing between tiers. More expensive plans might give you access to the greater speeds and reliability of the fast lane, while more affordable plans could be slower and less reliable.

This sort of tiered plan divides the Internet into two internets: an elite and privileged one and a limited one.

With a majority of people using the Internet, this creates a split in how well people are able to be informed about the world. Already (as of 2013) 26 million Americans are not able to afford access to the Internet, let alone being able to afford access to a top-tier (Merchant, 2013). Affordable or not, ISPs have been caught prioritizing network upgrades in wealthier neighborhoods. Those who live in neighborhoods ISPs consider poor or less profitable could find themselves without even availability of the fast lane in the first place due to slower, aging infrastructure.

Tiers, while providing yet another possible gap between the privileged and the underprivileged, would most likely be limited to speeds and wouldn't block content outright. While tiers are often compared to cable packages—in which more channels are available with a more expensive package—the analogy doesn't quite work. It appears unlikely that a provider would outright block access to sites on a tiered Internet, unless they can force services to exist in only one tier or another. Regardless of the form tiers come in, ISP could get to decide your level of privilege.

It doesn't take much to change people's online behavior. Simply by slowing services down or introducing caps on data used that doesn't fall under a customer's plan, service providers can effectively discourage people from visiting them. There's a lot more on the Internet than many people realize—everything from news, to source code, to online courses—parts of which many people may not use. The problem is, by discouraging use of those less common places, it becomes harder to get a view of what's going on a wider scale. Worse, it makes it more difficult to learn something new, outside of your current areas of expertise.

By encouraging some services over others—by allowing them to work better by being in the fast lane—problems with competition and independent creators appear. New competitors and Indie publishers are much less likely to be able to afford the benefits of being in the faster tier. ISPs could even mandate that high bandwidth services, like streaming video or telephone, operate in the higher tier so they can charge them more for the bandwidth they're using. Doing so would likely further entrench already-large services over smaller competition.

If a site lacked the funding to pay for its service to be part of the open Internet or an Internet fast lane, that service could be doomed to fail. Research from Microsoft suggests that slowing down a website by just 250ms (the blink of an eye) makes users more likely to use a competitor (Lohr, 2012). What that means for the owner of a small business or a personal website who can't pay to be in one of the so-called "fast lanes" is that they could encounter much more difficulty in keeping visitors. Large companies have the ability to pay the fees to be carried in those fast lanes which right away makes their voice stronger than others. Your voice, as well as the voice of your local community could easily be droned out by larger entities by even minuscule differences in speed. Any claims that a fast lane is only minutely faster should not, according to research, make being in the slow lane seem more acceptable.

To some degree a type of fast lane may be a necessary part of supporting high-bandwidth services. Netflix in particular is known for requiring massive amounts of bandwidth in order to support the streaming of HD and higher quality video. In 2015, it was reported that Netflix accounted for 37%—more than a third—of Internet bandwidth used during peak periods in North America (McAlone, 2015). This is an astounding amount of traffic for a single service to produce. To accommodate this, Netflix has agreements with ISPs which allows it to place servers on their networks. These hosting agreements place Netflix closer to its viewers while helping to lessen its bandwidth usage across the wider web, though also making it possible for Netflix's services to be a little faster.

Such agreements are not exclusive to Netflix. Much of the web is delivered by what are called CDNs (content delivery networks). While they have their own problems, CDNs allow often-used resources like images and icons to be served from ISP-shared servers. This allows upstream services to save on bandwidth costs by serving data to their customers from servers that are closer to their customers. To a large degree, this is a win for everyone. ISPs are able to save on bandwidth from the backbone providers they connect to, customers have faster access to certain data, and upstream services save money and bandwidth themselves.

Even if these fast-lanes exist only on the business side of the Internet rather than customer ISP plans, you could still be the one paying for them. In an ecosystem of digital fast lanes, services that choose or are required to pay to be carried in the faster tier would be likely to pass those costs onto their subscribers. The cost of bandwidth is already factored into the operating costs of services, and plays a role in their fees. More expensive bandwidth can lead to higher fees. ISPs justify this by complaining that content providers don't pay them—which is largely true—but content providers are paying for the bandwidth they use already just not to last-mile providers.

While net neutrality advocates are often convinced that tiers would be harmful to competition and to consumers, it's worth mentioning that it's possible they would be used very differently. In an IEEE interview, a net neutrality opponent suggests a very different possibility. Rather than dividing the Internet as net neutrality advocates fear, he suggests that a faster tier would mainly be used for specialized applications such as robotic surgery, which would be dependent on fast speeds and reliable connections, as well as others not yet imagined (Nordrum, 2017). Unfortunately, there is no way to know if this would be the case. Selling access to tiers, both to upstream content providers and to consumers could be a lucrative business for ISPs.

The technology to divide the Internet already exists and is widely available (even your home router likely supports some form of it). Typically, this would be used to allow VoIP (Internet telephone) to be given priority over other traffic so someone else loading a website doesn't cause call drops. Without net neutrality, service providers can use this to artificially limit speeds of certain sites or services based on the packages their customers subscribe to. This could mean that you would need to pay extra for gaming to be faster, or for the ability to work from home, or even just to have Skype work reasonably well. While service providers likely wouldn't block services altogether, a tiered Internet could be built around that sort of traffic shaping. There isn't a technological reason for providers to do this, based on what's known of their networks. Unfortunately, there's also no way to escape it as a customer because there are so few ISP options available.

For those who are unable to afford or who are unwilling to pay to use top-tier services, the two-lane Internet provides yet another expense for being poor or frugal. Companies could choose to recruit primarily in the upper tiers—if for no reason other than to show they could—leaving limited opportunities for applicants who don't have access. This creates yet another barrier for moving up in the world if you happen to be one of millions of low-income households. How much of the world you can be informed about and what sort of job opportunities are available to you could be determined by what tier you can pay for.

These differing access options also produce the illusion of being informed. Being unable to access or being deterred from accessing the whole Internet means the interest targeting of most websites becomes a much bigger problem. If websites can detect you're in a lower tier, they may also change how they present the world to you—something that they already do based on where you live.

Any sort of tiered Internet—whether it's driven by zero-rating or by fast lanes—creates an information divide. The practices are marketable ways of artificially creating scarcity and demand. Both limit your ability to access information based on what you're able or willing to pay your ISP every month and on what sort of agreements online services are willing to forge with your ISP to get their content to you. Based on that, you have access to only parts of the Internet depending if you're part of the informed elite, or the slower, limited tier. ISPs could take advantage of such a gap to divide people and to manipulate opinions.

. . .

THE FIGHT FOR THE INTERNET

13 · Telecom Lobbying

Data and communications companies have throughout history fought for more favorable regulations for themselves and have at times even manipulated elections by carefully controlling information. The internet industry is no exception, having demonstrated a notable lobbying muscle of its own. In 2014, the (known) amounts of money spent on lobbying for anti net neutrality causes amounted to $49,049,000 (Drutman & Furnas, 2016). In the first quarter of 2017 alone, over 11 million was spent on lobbying (Neidig, 2017).

Although it's typical for ISPs to claim otherwise, Telecom lobbying is not about serving customers better, it's about serving the business and its investors better. Depending on the company, ISPs have lobbied both for and against net neutrality. Large, national ISPs tend to lobby against neutrality. Certain others, such as Sprint, lobby for it (Lawler, 2015). The differences between these positions likely lie with the size of the company and the infrastructure they have available. Large internet providers have a lot of leverage in pushing higher pricing for moving data over their networks and are not reliant on other companies for their last mile offerings. In comparison, small carriers such as Sprint do not have that luxury. Such carriers may only be coincidentally in favor of net neutrality because neutrality supports their businesses by requiring larger carriers to sell network capacity that smaller carriers can use.

As a smaller wireless carrier, Sprint has more things working against it. The company does not have a wired business that can support its bottom line if its wireless network doesn't grow. Being smaller, it also has less leverage to force customers or upstream providers into different deals for moving data over their networks. Not only that, but Sprint shares network capacity with Verizon and AT&T, which allows the network to offer more coverage than Sprint's own infrastructure would otherwise allow. Net neutrality regulations that require infrastructure sharing therefore favor smaller carriers like Sprint. If allowed, larger networks that Sprint shares resources with would have better legal standing to increase prices more than Sprint could afford or forbid Sprint from sharing their network altogether (Reardon, 2015).

Telecom lobbying extends to a wide variety of things. The industry has lobbied to slide out of contracts by providing the bare minimum or less. It has lobbied to reduce privacy and transparency restrictions. ISP lobbyists have even claimed that the expectation they would provide wide-reaching networks was a "miscalculation" by the public when it came to rural areas. Of course, most ISPs also actively lobby against net neutrality Title II regulations.

As mentioned with ISPs using taxpayer-funded grants to expand their networks and tiptoeing their way around actually fulfilling the terms of those contracts, ISPs have lobbied their way out of promises. These have allowed various ISPs to do the bare minimum—which in some cases could be argued as being less than that—in order to keep the maximum amount of money from those grants themselves. Of course, lobbying to get those grants in the first place happened as well.

The fact that some ISPs have been resistant to or have completely avoided expanding their networks to serve rural areas has also been subject to ISP lobbying. According to the U.S. Internet Industry Association (USIAA), those who live in rural areas who do not have access have "miscalculated" in claims that America has failed in its efforts to bring the network to them. Rather, it claims that it isn't a failure of the ISPs, but it's because people are poor (Bode, 2008). Given that homegrown ISPs have surfaced to serve such areas, the claim that people don't want access or are unable to pay for it appears to be untrue.

Lobbying activities are met with enough success that

ISPs are willing to spend millions of dollars on them every quarter. Thanks to the efforts of Telecom lobbyists, Congress voted to weaken the FCC's authority to enforce regulations that support net neutrality. Most recently, ISP lobbyists won a victory against privacy regulations. Due to that victory, ISPs are now allowed to be more liberal with collection and use of online activities of their customers (Kang, 2017). Of course, ISPs frequently release statements that make it appear less like rulings such as those are caused in any way by ISPs. With their privacy victory, a number of ISPs put out statements—including various joint statements—pledging their commitment to customer privacy despite their role in the ruling.

Lobbying from ISPs takes a wide variety of forms. There are, of course, the typical Washington D.C. lobbyists who try to directly influence the policy making of the agencies who oversee their business. Lobbying of this form is difficult to know the full extent of, though third party organizations like The Sunlight Foundation and OpenSecrets attempt to make it more transparent. The smallest amount it took to convince a member of Congress to support the FCC's new proposal against net neutrality was $146,000, which is still above the average contributed to the cause (Noland, 2017).

Paid lobbying is not the only way ISPs attempt to push their agenda. Companies have also been accused of astroturfing, or attempting to hide the source of support for their cause by making it look like a grassroots movement. Astroturfing can be difficult to uncover because it doesn't always involve paid lobbying, and when done well is well hidden. ISPs have used their employees for the purpose, which is inexpensive for them because it doesn't involve any additional investment on their part.

The West Virginia Board of Utilities was lobbied this way. Using its employees to create the appearance of grassroots support, an ISP was successful in convincing the board that the terms of a network expansion agreement did not require the network builder to actually connect anything to its network, but that it only required it to run new fiber down streets.

In 2009, another internet service provider attempted a similar strategy. The company's top lobbyist emailed all 300,000 employees at the time asking them to leave comments for the FCC against net neutrality rules on wireless networks and to encourage their friends and family to do the same. Talking points to bring up to the FCC were also suggested, including such thing as "competition in the mobile industry is strong" and "net neutrality rules could hamper a goal of the White House to bring broadband to every U.S. household." It was suggested that employees hide their company affiliation by using a personal email rather than a business one (Kang, 2009). While the email could read as a suggestion, it's a little difficult to see it as such with the context of it being sent from a top executive at the company.

More recently, with the 2017 comment period for the FCC's plan to dismantle net neutrality, similar odd practices have appeared. While they haven't been tied to ISPs, their prevalence was somewhat striking. Bots, who were easy to spot due to their use of alphabetically organized names and identical or very similar comments, left thousands of anti net neutrality comments on the proposal. Further observation discovered that comments opposed to net neutrality were also being posted by dead people (Oberhaus, 2017) and impersonated living people (Fung, 2017b). The intent was clearly to tip the balance of the comments towards an anti net neutrality sentiment. Given the popular opinion in favor of net neutrality such a large and targeted effort is a little suspicious, though not necessarily improbable from certain online communities. It's worth noting that, to a lesser degree, there have been fake comments in favor of net neutrality as well (Snider, 2017) so neither side is entirely without fault in the comment war.

Telecom lobbying, in all forms, does not appear to be slowing down. As of April 2017, reports from the Senate Office of Public Records showed that telecoms had already spent over twenty million dollars on lobbying efforts (Lobbying Spending Database, n.d.). With victories such as the repeal of ISP privacy regulations, ISPs have no reason to stop. Further, with the massive public support for net neutrality, which most large ISPs are vehemently against, lobbying efforts are likely to step up in the fight against it—convincing both the public and the government that Title II is a bad idea.

Perhaps most offensively is that ISP lobbying doesn't stop at things that directly affect their own business— things like fighting net neutrality or avoiding providing networks in areas that would be less profitable. In 2005, two large ISPs denied claims that they had pushed to prevent communities from building municipal networks. However, they claimed that they had and would continue to push to prevent cities from building their own broadband services—but only due to regulations that were trying to be imposed on them. However, those efforts have happened in nearly every state, even for areas where those ISPs did not express interest in operating in (Bode, 2005).

This sort of lobbying is expensive to taxpayers for multiple reasons. The most direct outcome is that it has left people unable to get online for no technological reason other than ISPs not wanting to provide service to their area. Networks capable of being used for municipal broadband that were paid for by taxpayers exist in hundreds of cities. However, ISPs have lobbied to prevent them from ever being used by the public. Telecoms themselves have refused to use this infrastructure, despite complaining that building infrastructure is expensive (Connolly, 2014). These networks could connect people to a much faster, more reliable Internet for far less cost. However, it would cut into the bottom line of big ISPs who would prefer you to use their services instead. Suing cities that have created or intend to create municipal broadband service is not unheard-of either (Comcast Sues EPB, 2008).

Where lobbying is allowed, it's not unreasonable for companies to push for changes favorable to their business. However, the amount of money spent on preventing taxpayer-funded infrastructure from being used and pushing for anti-consumer practices is a huge loss for the end user. The 20 million dollars spent convincing the FCC and representatives for policy changes could have gone instead towards improving networks and providing Internet to more people. Unfortunately, ISPs have managed to influence the creation of laws restricting or forbidding municipal broadband networks in 20 states (Cox, 2014), which could provide better prices. Telecoms have also manipulated privacy, competition, and neutrality agreements through lobbying efforts. These practices are rarely in the best interest of the Internet or its users.

. . .

14 · Regulation

The primary discussion of regulation with regard to net neutrality centers around the FCC. The FCC, or Federal Communications Commission, is a government agency in the United States that deals with interstate communications in terms of telephone, television, broadband Internet, public safety, and management of wireless resources. Its mission, paraphrased, is to make wire and wireless communication services available to all citizens, regardless of who they are, at a reasonable price. In order to do that, they have jurisdiction over communication mediums (such as radio bands).

The FCC has its own board and voting process for putting in place or repealing the regulations that govern telecommunications and doesn't require approval from Congress. However, the agency is required to take into account public opinion, and most proposals collect public comment during the voting process. Unfortunately, the FCC is subject to lobbying and tends to align with the political ideas of the White House so the degree to which public opinion is observed in their proceedings tends to vary. Observed or not, the sentiment of public feedback on FCC proceedings can be used in court against FCC decisions.

In 2015, the FCC classified ISPs as information services under Title II. This classification gives the FCC authority to regulate ISPs in order to protect their customers. Title II and Section 706 are two of the main regulations associated with protecting net neutrality. Both require enforcement in order to be effective, something that has been lacking in the past. These regulations prevent ISPs from prioritizing certain content over others, violating customer privacy, or censoring online content they disagree or compete with. Putting in place and enforcing net neutrality regulations is required for keeping the Internet a neutral and open flow of information.

Title II of the Communications Act of 1934 says that internet service providers are not allowed to (among other things) "make any unjust or unreasonable discrimination in charges, practices, classifications, regulations, facilities, or services." It further prevents service providers from discriminating against different content types for any reason, which is important for protecting ISP customers from things like paid prioritization, encouraging some services over others, or censoring websites the ISP disagrees with. This is important given the media affiliations of many ISPs and how much control they can exert since they've become gatekeepers to the information found online.

While Title II is referred to somewhat generically for net neutrality, the FCC outlined specifically what parts of it will be applied to ISPs. The regulations in place under Title II are considered "light-touch" and exclude over 700 rules from the full Title II regulation. The rules that would be applied to ISPs can be boiled down to a few basic things: no blocking, no throttling, and no paid fast lanes. A few others would be examined individually if issues were to come up, such as disputes over the point where last-mile networks connect to the Internet backbone. Reasonable network maintenance is also allowed, but requires a technical justification rather than a business one (Kastrenakes, 2015).

The Title II regulations put in place are good at allowing the FCC jurisdiction in making sure the Internet business is allowed to evolve, while bringing along appropriate amounts of competition and consumer protection. It does not attempt to prevent ISPs from building out their networks to better support new high-bandwidth applications. ISPs would have the public believe that net neutrality would prevent their networks from evolving, though this is untrue with Title II type regulations. Equal access to information is what net neutrality provides—not restrictions on how a network can be managed (Zhang, Mao, & Zhang, 2008).

Section 706 of the same act would go further if implemented, allowing the FCC to use regulation to promote competition in the market as well as to regulate telecom infrastructure more closely. Competition is another important part of net neutrality, since it provides business incentives for providing good service at reasonable prices. Given the price drops and improvements that service providers seem able to pull out of thin air in response to competition, it's clear that they are capable of offering better rates and service than they do. Although the effects of Google Fiber haven't been felt in much of the country, the ongoing battle for the best "unlimited" plan has or likely will be. In 2017 there was an ongoing push from multiple mobile data providers pushing for the most "unlimited" "unlimited" plan, if their advertising is to be believed. This sort of competition is good for consumers who then have more options and better prices. When sudden competition can drive down costs so much, it's clear that the current free market system is not working as it should. ISPs get wealthier, while their customers find higher prices and lower quality of service.

The reason regulations are more necessary now than they were previously is that the last mile ecosystem has changed. The Internet hasn't always been a place of large telecoms. In its early days, access was provided by many small, independent service providers and the market was far more competitive. The Internet was a novelty, so choosing to simply not be online was a viable option if you disagreed with your ISP's practices. The ISP market is very different now, and is run by a much smaller group of much more powerful companies.

Verizon, AT&T, Comcast, and other large providers have been outspoken about their opposition to being regulated under Title II classification and Section 706. Verizon even floated the claim that Title II would change how it invested in improvements to its infrastructure. At face value, these concerns are valid. Service providers still need control over their networks so they can continue to grow and evolve to support a changing Internet. Verizon and AT&T actually both agreed with net neutrality for broadband networks in 2008—although they were opposed to applying the same regulations to their wireless networks (Reardon, 2008).

In actuality, the impact of Title II regulations have not been nearly so severe. Comcast has admitted that net neutrality regulations are not the problem that it and other service providers have claimed they would be. Comcast defended its public opposition as a fear of the unknown, not knowing what Title II would actually mean for business (Cox, 2016). Sprint, the outlier of large ISPs even spoke out in favor of the Title II regulations.

Verizon's Chief Financial Officer (CFO) made a similar statement to investors prior to being classified under Title II, saying that Title II wouldn't hurt network investments. He quickly tried to backtrack on the statement after.

"I mean to be real clear, I mean this does not influence the way we invest. I mean we're going to continue to invest in

our networks and our platforms, both in Wireless and Wireline FiOS and where we need to. So nothing will influence that. I mean if you think about it, look, I mean we were born out of a highly regulated company, so we know how this operates." (Bode, 2014)

The legislative battle for the Internet is similar in many ways to legislative battles over cable TV and telephone, which provide a way to see some possibilities of a future with and without net neutrality. Telephone service over the majority of the United States was provided by a single company called Bell System that exerted full control over the telephone lines. They were effectively a monopoly. In order to connect something to a telephone line, even in your own home, you needed approval from the phone company. Often, you rented telephone equipment from the same company. The company was broken up in the 1980s and several regulations followed that provide the more open and non-discriminatory system that exists today.

Cable TV, on the other hand, went the opposite direction and provides service split into "packages" of different channels which sometimes disappear due to disagreements between cable providers and the broadcasting network—the reason why WFSB recently disappeared from Optimum customers in Connecticut (Turmelle, 2017), and why The Weather Channel disappeared from DirecTV. A non-neutral Internet is likely to look more like cable TV with similar disputes and higher prices.

Ignoring the possible problems of the effects of overly heavy-handed regulations on the Internet would be remiss. Bureaucracy is neither known for its speed nor its ability to stay current. Net neutrality regulations that are too stringent could result in the U.S. falling behind in information access for a different set of reasons than a lack of neutrality. The Internet has been able to evolve as quickly as it has because there have neither been regulations on what services could exist nor on how they could function. That has given ISPs the freedom to shape their networks as needed to match higher bandwidth needs and different types of services. ISPs still need the ability to manage their networks, or the next evolution of Netflix could bring infrastructure to a crawl while networks are held back by the legislative process. Overly heavy-handed regulations could also prevent ISPs from protecting their networks from malware and illegal activities, something the Title II rules ensure ISPs are able to do.

Despite being the bureaucratic monsters they tend to be, governments are good at ensuring people have fair and reliable access to utilities. With the scale of the companies that provide Internet access, the power to ensure fair and equal access is not in the hands of customers. The government needs to step in and regulate access as a utility. The ISP industry has been plagued by broken promises and rising prices. At this point, equal and reliable access to the Internet can only be guaranteed with regulations like Title II.

Unfortunately, precedent has shown that the FCC's stances on controversial issues like net neutrality can be impermanent. Leadership of the agency is appointed by the White House, and typically aligns with the political leanings of the current administration.

Under President Obama the FCC head was Tom Wheeler, named as head in 2013. Wheeler was a venture capitalist and lobbyist for the cable and wireless industry, which was not a fact that net neutrality advocates accepted easily on the understandable assumption that he had vested interests in the industry. However, Wheeler redeemed himself by classifying the Internet under Title II, the main tenet of net neutrality. In response to the surprise of both net neutrality advocates and the telecom industry, Wheeler explained that he was a supporter of the underdog, which during his lobbying days was the cable industry, but during his tenure at the FCC was net neutrality (Brodkin, 2016b). Under the oversight of Wheeler and the Obama administration, proponents of net neutrality, net neutrality advocates were hopeful that the battle would finally be put to rest.

That position has not held with the Transition from Obama to Trump. Trump named Ajit Varadaraj Pai head of the FCC in 2017. Pai served as Associate General Counsel at Verizon prior to being appointed to the FCC by Obama. Since his appointment, he has held various roles within the agency. He is known for being staunchly anti net neutrality, arguing that there is plenty of competition in the ISP space, that there is too much regulation, and that net neutrality is a mistake for consumers, despite evidence to the contrary. Popular opinion and several ISPs disagree with most of his positions. Despite that and overwhelmingly pro net neutrality comments left on the FCC's proposal to dismantle net neutrality, the FCC voted against Title II classification in May 2017. The outcome of that is yet to be seen, pending another vote and the changes taking effect later in the year. Under Pai, the net neutrality fight looks bleak with the FCC appearing to blatantly ignore public opinion and vote in the interests of the cable lobby. Pai has even gone so far as to refer to net neutrality as "a mistake" and has quoted Emperor Palpatine from Star Wars in his description of the regulations (Fiegerman, 2017). Public opinion is against him, but the FCC appears poised to push the net neutrality battle to a much longer and harder fight by ignoring that public opinion and inviting judicial challenges.

Another problem the FCC has had in preserving net neutrality is enforcement. FCC penalties for violating net neutrality regulations have been fairly minimal where they are listed at all. Previous legal precedents even say that ISPs don't need to pay fines they weren't warned about—which means even when the FCC chooses to impose penalties, because there are no specific penalties in the regulations, ISPs can easily avoid them (Liptak, 2012). Service providers already work around those penalties by carefully wording practices like zero-rating, explaining data caps as network constraints, and by lobbying Congress. Indeed, Congress even voted to strip the FCC of some of its authority to police net neutrality policies (The ISP Column, 2014).

In order to ensure that net neutrality remains a policy of the U.S., Congress needs to take Title II further and produce legislation that protects it. FCC changes and lobbying make it difficult to guarantee that net neutrality protections remain in place. Other countries, including Canada and Mexico have already made net neutrality principles into permanent legislative structures. Involvement from Congress, and hopefully forward-looking legislation on the subject, would move the epicenter of net neutrality regulations away from the FCC.

Unfortunately, Congress has prioritized other things over net neutrality, despite vocal opposition to much of their Internet policy and vocal support for net neutrality. The government branch has not shown a large degree of technical prowess when it has come to technology related legislation.

Previous congressional legislation regarding the Internet has also generally been disappointing. SOPA and PIPA, two bills aimed at stopping online privacy through the censoring of websites pushed for by Hollywood, appeared in 2012. These two bills, if passed, would have been highly damaging to net neutrality because they would have allowed intellectual property owners and Congress to blacklist websites that allegedly were involved in piracy. This type of legislation is often far from innocent. While one would hope that such a power wouldn't get misused to the degree that Turkey's online morality protections have been due to the protections on free speech and freedom of the press in the U.S., it opens the door for further censorship. SOPA and PIPA were scrapped after a massive online outcry which involved websites censoring themselves for a day (SOPA/PIPA, n.d.).

Support for net neutrality in Congress appears to be a partisan issue. Democrats have promised to wage war to protect the neutral Internet. However, the 2017 Republican controlled Congress has already voted against privacy protections enacted in 2015, and the aligning FCC is opposed to net neutrality (Reardon, 2017). Whether net neutrality will be protected by Congress is yet to be seen, but many organizations are gearing up for lawsuits to fight against a closed Internet.

. . .

15 · Municipal Internet

Municipal Internet—or, depending on the technology, "municipal fiber" or "municipal broadband"—refers to Internet service delivered by a local government agency or utility company. These services are usually funded in part by taxpayers, but typically also have subscription fees so that those interested in being connected to the network contribute more to its success. Being run from a local level allows service and pricing to be set up in ways to better suit the needs of the community the network operates in and to allow the network focus on improving local lives. Generally, municipal networks are structured and run more like a utility than an ISP because they answer directly to the communities they serve.

Municipal networks can take a few different forms, depending on the needs of the community and the funding available. The least expensive, of course is wireless. City-provided WiFi (or similar technologies) provide Internet access, usually with a series of WiFi re-transmitting devices, which accept a WiFi signal and re-broadcast it in order to extend its range. These networks, when built correctly, can be reliable, and are relatively inexpensive because there is little expensive digging and construction required to build a network. The more expensive but somewhat superior option is a more typical wired or fiber network to connect homes and businesses. This type of network requires expensive installation, but is more reliable, much faster, and can carry much more traffic.

While net neutrality typically focuses on municipal broadband that's offered to residents of a community, municipal networks are not always open to the public. Some networks serve only public buildings and services, which can include public schools and libraries, or can be limited to safety and federal officials. These restricted networks are often used to link traffic signals with each other and a central command center. While the average resident doesn't have access to these networks, they still benefit from them. Automated traffic control systems can keep traffic flowing efficiently. Reliable, fast networks can help emergency response crews in a disaster by giving them fast access to security cameras, communication, and other information they may need.

The public municipal networks net neutrality focuses on may provide those same services, but are also available as a local ISP option. This type of municipal network provides an alternative way to get online. Rural areas that traditional telecoms are not interested in serving can get access through a community broadband project, and others gain an alternate option. Public broadband projects provide a number of advantages to communities that choose to adopt them.

While some complain that municipal Internet raises taxes—if the network is taxpayer funded—it often saves the community money in the long run. Municipal broadband tends to be far less expensive than large ISPs while providing superior service.

Chattanooga, Tennessee, an often cited example of a successful municipal network, has a fiber network operated by a local power company. They offer a 100Mbps/100Mbps base package—which is ten times faster (or more) than the majority of the Internet access in the United States for $57 per month (EPB, 2017). That price is less than what Comcast charged for the same download speed but a slower upload speed ("Performance Pro Internet" plan) in some areas in early 2017, and in places where there are similar prices, there are data caps that apply (which raise the cost-per-gigabyte of service substantially). Spectrum's closest competing package the same year was the same price, but with a ten times slower upload speed. Sandy, Oregon offers municipal broadband as well, charging $40 for similar service. Other municipal governments provide Internet access free of charge based on income levels, or even to everyone.

Providing affordable Internet is important for ensuring equality and bringing people closer together. The ability to access the same information and opportunities as the rest of the population is a necessity for improving life. As the Chattanooga mayor explained,

"Our fiber goes to each and every home. We can't have digital gated communities. If we do that we and only allow fiber to go to some parts of the city, some parts of the state, we will see technology widen the gulf between people as opposed to bridging it." (McGee, 2016)

Communities with municipal networks, such as Chattanooga, often see a boom in business when the networks become available. The availability of inexpensive, reliable Internet service makes cities more appealing to businesses. Chattanooga experienced an economic revival after building its network, seeing unemployment rates in the city drop from 7.8% to 4.1%, and the wages of workers increase. The city has seen its number of downtown residents double and its landlords now offer apartments that include Internet access as part of their amenities, at no extra cost. The city, which was not a place anyone would have considered high tech, even has its own tech startup accelerator (McGee, 2016).

From a funding perspective, cities have an advantage over private ISPs. Governments are able to take a longer term view of investments, because they don't need to show profits to investors over a very short period. This allows networks to be developed and the costs written off over a longer term. Communities can develop broadband networks in pieces as the community can afford them, such as by piggybacking their installation off of existing infrastructure projects. Monroe County, New York has done this, installing fiber lines as digging for sewer, water, and other projects has been done. This was advantageous because the main cost of installing a fiber network is the cost of digging rather than the cost of the fiber. Monroe County's network is not a public ISP network, but appears to have the capacity to be used that way if the local government so chooses (Barnhart, 2015).

Not all municipal networks are taxpayer funded. Sandy, Oregon is such a network. Instead of being funded by tax dollars, the network was funded by revenue bonds. Ongoing profits are reinvested back into keeping access to the network affordable (Institute for Local Self Reliance, 2015). As the mayor explained, *we didn't feel it was right for everyone to have to pay for something that maybe not everyone was going to participate in.*

If a public network is not the only Internet option in an area, it helps to increase competition in the local ISP market. This helps bring down prices and helps push for better networks. Municipal networks can even help traditional telecoms expand their networks. Public networks don't have to be and are not always built for exclusive use. In some cases, they can be shared between multiple providers, which allows for more options than just the municipal one. Shared lines also allow for the cost of upgrades and maintenance to be spread between providers, which helps keep customer rates low.

Additional competition as well as a municipal option are important for ensuring a community's Internet needs are actually met. Typical large telecoms serve such wide areas that they don't care much for the individual communities they happen to serve. At times, they've even made community networks worse. It can be difficult to get large telecoms to hear and to address local needs, especially in rural areas which are often under served. San Francisco, a city in Silicon Valley, has different needs than a town in rural Maine. San Francisco likely has more employees who telecommute and more intensive bandwidth needs to service corporate offices of large online companies. Rural Maine meanwhile likely needs longer runs of infrastructure to service far fewer customers who use the web very differently.

A great example of addressing actual local needs is a look at the usefulness of "Cable WiFi" hotspots which some ISPs are rolling out. The hotspots are convenient because they're inexpensive for ISPs to run and available to any cable company customers in range. In a more densely populated area, these WiFi networks are almost ubiquitous and some providers such as Altice's Optimum even offer wireless phone service with them. However, in an area where buildings may be less dense, it's much more difficult if not impossible to build a functioning wireless network in the same way. More tech-oriented customers that can be found in an area like San Francisco are also likely more opposed to their Internet provider borrowing their home WiFi to provide a service they most likely don't use at home themselves.

ISPs have even been claimed to charge upwards of $20,000 to connect properties to their networks (Brodkin, 2014c), where they don't refuse to provide service in the first place. Areas where building a network is not worth the profits an ISP would make back from it makes the area somewhere where it's hard to convince a telecom to expand. Fortunately, municipal and homegrown ISPs have sprung up to fill the gap.

Municipal Internet projects are not always without problems. Building a network is expensive— Chattanooga's foray into municipal broadband came at a price tag of $330 million (McGee, 2016). There have been failed projects at large taxpayer expense, even with the best of intentions. Where funding isn't a problem, telecoms have managed to throw up legal hurdles by lobbying the FCC and local governments.

In 2004, Philadelphia began one of the first major municipal broadband ventures in the country, Wireless Philadelphia, run by a dedicated nonprofit. ISPs became concerned with the prospect of competing with a public network, and began lobbying for harder regulations on such projects. Although Philadelphia was able to work around the new hurdles, local politicians wanted to limit the city's involvement with the project. The reservations of those politicians led to a deal with EarthLink to build the network, which eventually resulted in EarthLink owning the network itself. Ultimately, EarthLink was not able to finish the network and in 2008, conceded failure and withdrew their involvement. Some suggest that the failure was due to the network being ahead of its time and technology, rather than the project itself being flawed. (Abraham, 2015)

An oft-cited and expensive municipal broadband failure is the UTOPIA project in Utah. From the beginning, the network had problems with construction planning, management, and use of its funding. The network missed its subscriber goals repeatedly and had a net loss, causing the cities involved to pay a collective $13 million a year just to pay back the bonds used to fund the project. (Page, 2012)

The use of taxpayer money in some municipal broadband projects, and the expense of some of the failures, may have given rise to the misconception that net neutrality involves providing free Internet access with tax dollars. Net neutrality itself does not mean forcing ISPs to provide free service or for tax dollars to be used to make the Internet free for everyone. While there are government subsidies for helping low-income households connect, these have been in place for some time. Subsidies can help bridge the digital gap alongside net neutrality, but are not part of net neutrality itself. Net neutrality is about requiring ISPs to provide equal access to the entire Internet if you pay for a connection. This means that no matter where you go online, be it at home, on the go, at a public library, or anywhere else, you can expect to be able to access the same sites at the same speed (limited of course only by the connection speed). This is a similar expectation to using a telephone at any of those same places—equal ability to call anyone on Earth no matter where the phone is. Whether a municipal network chooses to provide access for its community at no cost is the business of the community that owns it, not the general taxpayer.

An estimated 500 communities have built municipal broadband services (Community Broadband Networks, n.d.). It's clear that these projects are not unheard-of. In 2000, the FCC even endorsed municipal broadband as a way to bring the Internet to underserved communities (FCC, 2000). As technology improves, especially with regard to wireless, municipal networks using alternate networking options will become more affordable and more viable options for providing access on a wide scale.

Municipal networks are an important part of the net neutrality discussion because they provide more choices and therefore, more competition. By treating the Internet more like a utility, access can be more fair and more affordable, without content prioritization. In theory, more competition in the ISP space should make providers less likely to provide unfair pricing or non neutral practices. However, should that not be the case, municipal ISPs answer directly to the communities they serve, on a much smaller scale than traditional telecoms, which provides better transparency and accountability.

. . .

16 · Alternative Networks

As the Internet has grown, more possibilities for accessing it have been developed. Some are, for the layperson, somewhat mundane such as the ever-evolving mobile data network that powers cell phones that most are accustomed to using. Others are fodder for research and idealized alternate networking plans, such as mesh and peer to peer networks which while effective, generally operate on a small scale. Still others power what's referred to as "the dark web," a place where anonymity reigns. These alternate networks provide ways for net neutrality to flourish without input from ISPs or the FCC.

These networks are often community-operated so they are not in the hands, at least not directly, of ISPs who might be interested in taking part in practices that undermine net neutrality. They empower online users to own and run their own networks with the privacy and neutrality that people expect when they get online.

In some cases, they provide more possibilities for getting online for those who live in underserved rural areas or who are low-income and may not be able to afford a monthly bill from a normal ISP by offering alternate networks with different kinds of access plans.

An alternate network widely used for anonymity is Tor. The Tor network, an alternate Internet that runs over the existing Internet, is often referred to as "the dark web." The project was designed and partially funded by the U.S. Navy for covert communications. Tor traffic is difficult to track, both in terms of what the traffic contains as well as where it came from. While the network provides access to the normal Internet via the Tor network, there are websites that exist only within the network. Accessing the network requires the use of browser add-ons or specialized apps. The dark web connects with the rest of the Internet with servers referred to as Exit Nodes, which are run by volunteers around the world.

The anonymity that Tor provides helps support both licit and illicit activities. Within the Tor network are various activist and abuse survivor groups that can operate without censorship or concern for tracking. Law enforcement officials use the network in order to hide their originating network addresses so they can conduct searches without leaving traces of who they are. However, crime in the Tor network is also a problem. Drug deals, black market goods, and all manner of other criminal activity happen via Tor. Due to the anonymity that the network has and how difficult it is to track traffic—though it is possible and has been done in the past—Tor has been referred to as a truly free network.

Net neutrality violations do not affect the Tor network in the same way as the normal Internet. Due to how it works, ISPs can't actually examine traffic on the network. Traffic that leaves the Tor network—to connect to the online world outside of Tor—doesn't do so from the location it came from. This makes it impossible to uniformly throttle a particular type of traffic or content arriving through Tor, so fast lanes and zero rating don't work. In order to effectively implement such practices, all ISPs would need to agree on the same fast lanes and zero-rating, otherwise only some parts of the Tor network would be affected.

Tor is a type of network called a mesh network, although it isn't the type of infrastructure most imagine when discussing the technology. Mesh networks are collections of connected devices that provide access to the network (and possibly the Internet) to each other without a typical ISP. This type of network doesn't rely on only a single Internet connection, if it relies on one at all. Anyone who joins the network expands it, without necessarily requiring a wired or wireless ISP of their own. If you're part of a mesh network, people access web by passing traffic through your devices and the devices of anyone else in range, and you access the web by passing traffic through theirs. There are a few mesh networking services which are free, which improve availability of online opportunities for people who are not able to afford a traditional ISP.

Mesh networks are used in a variety of settings, usually where running cables to provide service is impractical or too expensive. This can include anything from rural areas where the cost of investing in a network couldn't easily be made back due to the lower density of users, or a building that wants to provide wireless coverage without lengthy renovations. Many mesh projects are mostly experimental, though there are some that exist and that are used outside of research. Some mesh networks are transparent. WiFi systems used in hospitality—that is, for guests in hotels and restaurants—sometimes use commercial products to connect WiFi nodes to the Internet without running cables all of them. Others require the use of dedicated software and devices.

Research into mesh networks was the beginnings of Meraki, bought by networking behemoth Cisco in 2012. Meraki began with a research network at MIT called Roofnet. The network had 20 active nodes on the network at one point according to its website (retrieved from the Internet Archive, as the project is no longer active). The goal of the project was to find better methods of handling network paths that are unreliable and developing new protocols for wireless technology.

Dedicated mesh networks, ones that do more than extend WiFi coverage, have been used to provide Internet service to rural areas and underserved towns.

Building a mesh network requires planning, but is not otherwise expensive. This allows the Internet to reach people who live too far for it to be cost-effective or affordable to build wired networks to them. Companies like StrixSystems build such networks. A case study on the company's website describes a network using mesh technologies that serves a population area of 100,000 people in Kentucky.

Although large mesh networks exist, for most people mesh networking is a largely do-it-yourself solution. How-to guides for getting started in building your own network are available online and in some cases are as easy to get started with as installing an app on your phone. Unfortunately, these home-grown networks based on consumer devices are limited by range and limited bandwidth that the devices support. They aren't, on a large scale, reliable replacements for a standard ISP. However, they often have communities that are enthusiastic about improving the technology. Most community mesh networking ventures are based on open source technologies meaning other networks are able to build on their work. PittMesh, a project in Pittsburgh, and Commotion Wireless, an open source mesh network tool, are two such open source projects.

Due to the fact that mesh networks circumvent local ISPs, they can help forward net neutrality by increasing competition and allowing households an escape from their one or two ISP choices. Should net neutrality regulations be repealed or undermined, having the option to find service elsewhere is important. Not all service providers allow sharing Internet connections in a way that supports mesh networks and doing so can get you disconnected or even banned from using their networks (particularly in the wireless market). However, on a large enough mesh network, everyone becomes their own ISP and that doesn't matter as much, so long as a connection to an ISP or backbone provider is in proximity to the network. As long as you're within range of the network, you have a connection.

The biggest problem with alternate Internet technologies, or building another Internet altogether, is adoption. Piggybacking on existing network technology is easy, which is what Tor and mesh networks do. However, convincing people to actually use the new network is entirely another story. The Internet as a universal communication tool makes it difficult to create independent networks that have access to some things, but not to the big services that everyone expects to be available. For mesh networks in particular, the network is much smaller and far less widespread with fewer users. That, in itself, makes it a less appealing network. Until enough early adopters join the network to make it useful, the rest of the online world won't follow.

On an Internet without neutrality, alternative networks may be more appealing to those otherwise unlikely to be early adopters. Throughout history, people have jumped from communication network to communication network as better access and ease of use have improved. It's possible that these alternative networks will be more appealing should the government continue to decline to maintain net neutrality. The hope is that different networks can limit or work around the damage done to the Internet through ISP profiteering.

. . .

17 · Taking Back the Internet

The most famed fight for an open network happened in the 1980s and resulted in the breakup of the Bell telephone monopoly. While the telephone is not the Internet, it provided a novel long-range communication service with access to various information services not entirely dissimilar from the Internet. The breakup of Bell bears a strong resemblance to the current fight to keep the Internet neutral.

Bell, at its peak, owned the entirety of long distance telephone lines in the United States. However, the company only serviced large population areas such as New York City and left rural areas disconnected from the network. These rural areas started their own phone companies by stringing lines to connect each other's houses, much like mesh networks. While some of these networks were fairly notable, they were not able to make long distance phone calls because they were not part of the larger Bell network. Building their own long distance infrastructure was out of the question for them due to the prohibitive costs of construction and maintenance. However, these independent networks still provided useful services, such as weather reports, even though their reach was limited.

Bit by bit, Bell absorbed these networks into the larger Bell network through various arrangements. While some preferred to remain independent, staying independent was difficult when it meant being disconnected from the larger network. The only options were to find a way into the Bell network or be tacitly excluded. Networks that were unwilling to make agreements with Bell were disconnected and increasingly isolated as the network grew around them, cutting them off from the rest of the world (Wu, 2012).

Laying long lines for communication remains an expensive task and indeed, only a handful of backbone providers exist who maintain long stretches of cable across the United States and across the ocean. When one of those providers experiences problems, large sections of the Internet can be disconnected from each other. Fortunately, as the network has grown, there are now multiple ways to get from point A to point B so a backbone outage may not disconnect people entirely—though it may slow down access to certain websites. Most large websites are distributed between multiple geographic areas to minimize the impact, but smaller ones don't always have that luxury.

The idea of "net neutrality" as the concept in the news

today is relatively new. However, the fight for net neutrality has been raging, in some form or another, for as long as humans have realized the benefits of long-range communication technologies. Guaranteeing that the information traveling over these networks can't be censored and can't be throttled has always been important. From Telegraph to Telephone, Radio to Television, and now the Internet, making sure large companies don't control what you're able to know is important.

The web was never intended to be tiered or restricted by the companies providing access to it. Its creator, Tim Berners-Lee, argues that the Internet should be an open flow of information where ISPs are not allowed to impose their will on their users, stressing that people need to have control over their information (Scott, 2014). Some shaping of that flow may a necessity to keep everything running smoothly, but zero-rating, data caps, and content shaping as implemented are not in any way required to keep the Internet running smoothly.

To that end, the FCC classified Internet providers under Title I in 2002, an "Information Service" classification. This is generally regarded as a win for net neutrality advocates but didn't go as far as many wanted. Title I classification has been referred to as a "hands off" or "lite" classification in that it recognized that the Internet was an important means of communication but provided minimal regulation around that status. The classification allowed the FCC some indirect authority to regulate interstate and international communications online, but didn't allow regulation of services themselves. While the FCC promised that Title I would allow them to enforce net neutrality as needed, Title I by its definition did not allow them to follow up on those promises (Miranda, 2013).

ISPs fought Title I classification and rightly won against the FCC in court in late 2013. They argued that by the FCC's own definition of the classification, the FCC was not permitted to regulate them because their Title I violations that did not happen on an interstate or international level. The long-term outcome of the win was a formal declaration that ISPs would need to be classified under Title II if the FCC wanted to impose the regulations they promised (Miranda, 2013). In 2015, the FCC did just that (Chappell, 2015).

Title II gives the FCC authority to protect ISP customers from "unjust" practices such as discrimination against certain content types, among other things. It also gives the FCC the ability to enact policies that would encourage and expand competition in the Internet provider industry. Both of these are key for protecting net neutrality. Articles claiming that Title II was the nightmare of ISPs appeared en masse, but in actuality there was minimal business impact. Sprint even came out in favor of Title II classification. That is not to say that ISPs are not continuing to fight against net neutrality in every way they can because they are, and with alarming degrees of success.

Due to the ongoing fight, net neutrality has never been fully secure. Despite advocates' best efforts to be heard which in both 2014 (Kastrenakes, 2014) and 2017 (Kastrenakes, 2017) gathered millions of comments in favor of net neutrality, Congress and some members of the FCC remain opposed to the idea. While disagreement is a healthy part of a democracy, the public opinion appears to be that the Internet should have neutrality protections (Brodkin, 2017a). However, Congress has voted to strip some FCC regulatory powers and the FCC under Pai laid out a plan to tear apart net neutrality.

From a non-legislative standpoint the fight against net neutrality continues as well. An ISP group began a misleading ad campaign in 2017 claiming support for net neutrality but without Title II classification, suggesting that the two could not be equated (Watson, 2017). One ISP published a video interview with its legal counsel explaining that net neutrality was at the forefront of its priorities but that the legislation for it was a mistake, though the claims were widely regarded as entirely false (Morran, 2017). There are cable-industry run websites that attempt to make a case for why net neutrality is a problem. Claims were made that ISPs would remain committed to customer privacy and to competition.

However, telecoms are often the ones fighting the privacy and neutrality regulations that they claim to be in favor of. That's not to mention that Title II equates to net neutrality according to the court ruling in the battle between the FCC and Verizon over Title I. Worse is the fact that telecoms have blatantly violated net neutrality principles in the past and now have the technology to do far worse in less obvious ways.

Internet providers and the FCC head, Pai, would have the public believe that a non-neutral web is in their best interest. The only hope of swaying public opinion is to convince the public that a non-neutral playing field is better for them and for business. Clever marketing of zero-rating as a great free way to have data forwards the ISP cause by making the start of a non neutral Internet seem like a sweet deal.

The FCC under Pai has even gone so far as to claim that the Internet is not a telecommunications service. Should this argument be successful, the FCC would have fewer obstacles to removing the Title II classification of internet service providers. This argument appears to be based on a misinterpretation of how the Internet works. However, the FCC is, according to legal precedent, allowed to change its interpretation of regulations as it sees fit (Brodkin, 2017b).

Net neutrality has been referred to as one of the most important digital rights battles of the Information Age. Regardless of beliefs, political standpoints, backgrounds, or any other facet, the outcome of net neutrality battles will impact everyone. The convenience and ubiquity of the Internet make it an increasingly critical resource for staying informed about the world and for validating that information no matter where it came from. This is not a fight anyone can afford to sit out of. Freedom of speech, the ability to be informed, the ability to be heard, and the ability to hear others is critical to society and to running a healthy democracy.

Telecoms have the placement and the technology to control what you can see. Leaving them with the ability to leverage that power is risky. There is, of course, the possibility that little will change and that Internet providers will act as benevolent gateways. However, the possibility that they won't be benevolent and neutral is too great a risk. As the country that created the Internet and that encourages democracy throughout the world, the United States needs to set a global example and protect the Internet from the companies that stand to gain the most from exerting deep control over its use. The pieces of both net neutrality and a divided Internet already exist; the policies that are adopted will determine the future of the Internet and of your ability to be informed.

# # #

Thank you for reading! If you enjoyed this book, or at the very least found it informative, please consider leaving a review at your favorite retailer. This book is independently published and is not backed by a marketing team. Your support makes indie books possible.

For more information about net neutrality as well as ways you can help support it, visit www.natelevesque.com/causes/net-neutrality   and consider supporting organizations such as the ACLU, EFF, and Fight For the Future.

Acknowledgments

This book was written with the support and understanding of a number of people.

Chelsea Eckert provided encouragement and convincing that I was, in fact, capable of writing a book that might not be nominated for the worst of the year. Hopefully, it is not nominated so I don't need to consider updating this page.

Seth Hendrick put up with delayed chores and dinners caused by a mad scramble to put as much forward progress into this book as possible on only nights and weekends. Special thanks is due for putting up with the musings and secrecy of a writer not yet ready to share a work while needing a sounding board for ideas, as well as for putting up with the general insanity of living with someone making a passionate effort to write a book.

Members of the Rochester Institute of Technology FOSS

(Free and Open Source Software) organization helped with vetting sources and providing feedback on advance copies of this book. Their help ensured the information in this book is accurate and understandable. Special thanks to Justin Flory for helping to get the message out.

~ ~ ~

About the Author

Nate Levesque is an alumni of the Rochester Institute of Technology Software Engineering program. He works as a full-time software engineer during the day. During his spare time on nights and weekends he writes and contributes to open source projects. He has a passion for free and open source software and digital rights.

You can learn more about Nate Levesque from his author profile on the Smashwords bookstore at www.smashwords.com/profile/view/thenaterhood.

For more things from Nate, including software projects, his personal blog, and other musings, visit www.natelevesque.com.

~ ~ ~

Bibliography

2015 Community Connect Broadband Grant Program Award Summaries. (2015). Retrieved April 29, 2017, from https://www.rd.usda.gov/files/UTP-CCProjectSummaries2015.pdf

Abraham, T. (2015, March 4). *What other cities should learn from Philly's failed municipal broadband effort*. Retrieved May 31, 2017, from https://technical.ly/philly/2015/03/04/cities-learn-phillys-failed-municipal-broadband-effort/

Akamai's [state of the Internet] Q1 2016 Report. (2016). Retrieved June 13, 2017, from https://www.akamai.com/us/en/multimedia/documents/state-of-the-internet/akamai-state-of-the-internet-report-q1-2016.pdf

Akgül, M. & Kırlıdoğ, M. (2015). *Internet censorship in Turkey*. Internet Policy Review, 4(2). DOI: 10.14763/2015.2.366

Anderson, N. (2009, June 3). *What a non-neutral 'Net looks like, UK-style*. Retrieved May 23, 2017, from https://arstechnica.com/tech-policy/2009/06/what-a-non-neutral-net-looks-like/

Anderson, N. (2012, December 18). *Report: data caps just a "cash cow" for Internet providers*. Retrieved May 23, 2017, from http://arstechnica.com/business/2012/12/report-data-caps-just-a-cash-cow-for-internet-providers/

Barnhart, R. (2015, February 23). *Taxpayer-Funded Fiber Lines Way Under Capacity*. Retrieved May 23, 2017, from http://www.rochesterfirst.com/news/news/taxpayer-funded-fiber-lines-way-under-capacity/190644358

Bode, K. (2005, March 17). *Verizon, SBC Chiefs play dumb*. Retrieved May 18, 2017, from http://www.dslreports.com/shownews/61506

Bode, K. (2008, March 6). *ISP Lobbying Group: What Rural Broadband Problem? - Move along folks, there's nothing to see here....* Retrieved May 23, 2017, from http://www.dslreports.com/shownews/ISP-Lobbying-Group-What-Rural-Broadband-Problem-92407

Bode, K. (2014, December 11). *Verizon Admits To Investors That Title II Won't Harm Broadband Investment At All*. Retrieved May 23, 2017, from https://www.techdirt.com/blog/netneutrality/articles/20141211/05462229389/verizon-admits-to-investors-that-title-ii-wont-harm-broadband-investment-all.shtml

Bode, K. (2016, July 22). *Lawsuit Claims Frontier Misused Millions In Federal Broadband Stimulus Funds*. Retrieved March 23, 2017, from https://www.techdirt.com/articles/20160721/10333935032/lawsuit-claims-frontier-misused-millions-federal-broadband-stimulus-funds.shtml

Bode, K. (2017, May 10). *Comcast, Charter Join Forces In Wireless, Agree Not To Compete*. Retrieved April 26, 2017, from https://www.techdirt.com/articles/20170509/052901373 22/comcast-charter-join-forces-wireless-agree-not-to-compete.shtml

Bohn, D. (2017, May 31). *Netflix CEO says net neutrality is 'not our primary battle'*. Retrieved June 2, 2017, from https://www.theverge.com/2017/5/31/15719824/netflix-ceo-reed-hastings-net-neutrality-not-our-battle

Brodkin, J. (2014a, April 6). *One big reason we lack Internet competition: Starting an ISP is really hard*. Retrieved May 23, 2017, from http://arstechnica.com/business/2014/04/one-big-reason-we-lack-internet-competition-starting-an-isp-is-really-hard/

Brodkin, J. (2014b, July 29). *ISPs tell government that congestion is "not a problem," impose data caps anyway*. Retrieved May 23, 2017, from https://arstechnica.com/business/2014/07/isps-tell-government-that-congestion-is-not-a-problem-impose-data-caps-anyway/

Brodkin, J. (2014c, November 5). *One man's failed quest to buy wired Internet from TWC or Verizon*. Retrieved May 23, 2017, from https://arstechnica.com/information-technology/2014/11/one-mans-failed-quest-to-buy-wired-internet-from-twc-or-verizon/

Brodkin, J. (2015a, April 13). *Google Fiber plans expansion, then TWC makes speeds six times faster*. Retrieved May 23, 2017, from http://arstechnica.com/business/2015/04/google-fiber-plans-expansion-then-twc-makes-speeds-six-times-faster/

Brodkin, J. (2015b, October 6). *How net neutrality violates the First Amendment (according to one ISP)*. Retrieved May 23, 2017, from https://arstechnica.com/tech-policy/2015/10/net-neutrality-violates-the-first-amendment-according-to-one-isp/

Brodkin, J. (2016a, February 5). *Verizon's mobile video won't count against data caps—but Netflix does*. Retrieved May 23, 2017, from http://arstechnica.com/business/2016/02/verizons-mobile-video-wont-count-against-data-caps-but-netflix-will/

Brodkin, J. (2016b, March 16). *How a former lobbyist became the broadband industry's worst nightmare*. Retrieved April 23, 2017, from https://arstechnica.com/business/2016/03/how-a-former-lobbyist-became-the-broadband-industrys-worst-nightmare/

Brodkin, J. (2016c, May 24). *Charter explains why it doesn't compete against other cable companies*. Retrieved May 23, 2017, from http://arstechnica.com/business/2016/05/charter-wont-compete-against-cable-firms-because-it-might-buy-them-later/

Brodkin, J. (2017a, May 15). *Flooded with thoughtful net neutrality comments, FCC highlights "mean tweets"*. Retrieved May 23, 2017, from https://arstechnica.com/tech-policy/2017/05/most-fcc-commenters-favor-net-neutrality-but-you-wouldnt-know-it-from-ajit-pai/

Brodkin, J. (2017b, June 1). *To kill net neutrality rules, FCC says broadband isn't "telecommunications"*. Retrieved June 1, 2017, from https://arstechnica.com/information-technology/2017/06/to-kill-net-neutrality-rules-fcc-says-broadband-isnt-telecommunications/

Brown, E., Snider, M., & Yu, R. (2015, February 24). *What is net neutrality and what does it mean for me?*. Retrieved May 23, 2017, from http://www.usatoday.com/story/tech/2015/02/24/net-neutrality-what-is-it-guide/23237737/

Chappell, B. (2015, February 26). *FCC Approves Net Neutrality Rules For 'Open Internet'*. Retrieved May 23, 2017, from http://www.npr.org/sections/thetwo-way/2015/02/26/389259382/net-neutrality-up-for-vote-today-by-fcc-board

Christian, T. (2015, February 16). *Web privacy is the newest luxury item in era of pervasive tracking*. Retrieved May 23, 2017, from http://www.csmonitor.com/World/Passcode/2015/0216/Web-privacy-is-the-newest-luxury-item-in-era-of-pervasive-tracking

Comcast Sues EPB In Hamilton County On Eve Of Bond Issue. (2008, April 22). Retrieved December 22, 2016, from http://www.chattanoogan.com/2008/4/22/126367/Comcast-Sues-EPB-In-Hamilton-County.aspx

Community broadband networks. (n.d.). Retrieved May 31, 2017, from https://muninetworks.org/communitymap

> This is an interactive map of municipal networks across the United States. Under the map is the number of community networks referenced in the text.

Connolly, M. (2014, June 5). *Buried Under Hundreds of Cities Is High-Tech Infrastructure Big Telecom Refuses to Use.* Retrieved December 22, 2016, from https://mic.com/articles/90523/buried-under-hundreds-of-cities-is-high-tech-infrastructure-big-telecom-refuses-to-use

Cox, K. (2014, August 28). *How ISPs "Compete" With Municipal Networks: Lobbying and Campaign Donations That Block Them.* Retrieved December 29, 2016, from https://consumerist.com/2014/08/28/how-isps-compete-with-municipal-networks-lobbying-and-campaign-donations-that-block-them/

Cox, K. (2016, December 9). *Comcast Exec Admits That Net Neutrality Is Not As Scary As Industry Made It Out To Be.* Retrieved May 23, 2017, from https://consumerist.com/2016/12/09/comcast-exec-admits-that-net-neutrality-is-not-as-scary-as-industry-made-it-out-to-be/

Cox, K. (2017, January 31). *Small Cable Companies, Indie Networks Ask FCC To Force Channel Unbundling.* Retrieved May 27, 2017, from https://consumerist.com/2017/01/31/small-cable-companies-indie-networks-ask-fcc-to-force-channel-unbundling/

Drutman, L., & Furnas, A. (2014, May 16). *How telecoms and cable have dominated net neutrality lobbying.* Retrieved May 23, 2017, from https://sunlightfoundation.com/2014/05/16/how-telecoms-and-cable-have-dominated-net-neutrality-lobbying/

Dugan, A. (2014, January 6). *Americans' Tech Tastes Change With Times*. Retrieved December 20, 2016, from http://www.gallup.com/poll/166745/americans-tech-tastes-change-times.aspx

Elgan, M. (2016, February 15). *The surprising truth about Facebook's Internet.org*. Retrieved May 23, 2017, from http://www.computerworld.com/article/3032646/intern et/the-surprising-truth-about-facebooks-internetorg.html

Engel, P. (2014, October 21). *Here's How Liberal Or Conservative Major News Sources Really Are*. Retrieved May 23, 2017, from http://www.businessinsider.com/what-your-preferred-news-outlet-says-about-your-political-ideology-2014-10

EPB. (2017). Internet. Retrieved May 23, 2017, from https://epb.com/home-store/internet

> This is the pricing page from EPB as it was on May 23, 2017. As this is a live pricing page, the rates advertised on it are subject to change as EPB sees fit.

Epstein, Z., Mills, C., Smith, C., & Wehner, M. (2015, November 19). *Comcast's data caps aren't just bad for subscribers, they're bad for us all*. Retrieved May 23, 2017, from http://bgr.com/2015/11/19/comcast-data-cap-2015-bad-for-us-all/

Fang, L. (2017, March 29). *Comcast-Funded Civil Rights Groups Claim Low-Income People Prefer Ads Over Privacy*. Retrieved April 3, 2017 from https://theintercept.com/2017/03/29/isp-civil-rights/

Feamster, N. (2016, February 10). *How Does Zero-Rating Affect Mobile Data Usage?*. Retrieved May 23, 2017, from https://freedom-to-tinker.com/2016/02/10/how-does-zero-rating-affect-mobile-data-usage/

Fiegerman, S. (2017, January 24). *The FCC's net neutrality fight is coming. Here's why it matters.* Retrieved May 23, 2017, from http://money.cnn.com/2017/01/24/technology/fcc-net-neutrality/index.html

Fight For The Future. (2017). *Comcast tries to censor pro-net neutrality website calling for investigation of fake FCC comments potentially funded by cable lobby* [Press release]. Retrieved from https://www.fightforthefuture.org/news/2017-05-23-comcast-tries-to-censor-pro-net-neutrality-website/

Friar, C., & Wyrich, A. (2017, May 23). *The history of net neutrality violations.* Retrieved May 23, 2017, from https://www.dailydot.com/layer8/net-neutrality-violations-history/

Fung, B. (2014, July 24). *ISPs are spending less on their networks as they make more money off them.* Retrieved February 6, 2017, from https://www.washingtonpost.com/news/the-switch/wp/2014/07/24/isps-are-spending-less-on-their-networks-as-they-make-more-money-off-them/

Fung, B. (2015, July 14). *Here's how data caps really affect your Internet use, according to data.* Retrieved May 23, 2017, from https://www.washingtonpost.com/news/the-switch/wp/2015/07/14/heres-how-data-caps-really-affect-your-internet-use-according-to-data/

Fung, B. (2017a, May 12). *Sprint and T-Mobile are reportedly in merger talks again.* Retrieved April 4, 2017, from https://www.washingtonpost.com/news/the-switch/wp/2017/05/12/sprint-and-t-mobile-are-reportedly-in-merger-talks-again/

Fung, B. (2017b, May 25). *Someone impersonated them to slam the FCC's net neutrality rules. Now they want answers*. Retrieved May 28, 2017, from https://www.washingtonpost.com/news/the-switch/wp/2017/05/25/somebody-impersonated-these-people-to-criticize-the-fccs-net-neutrality-rules-now-the-victims-are-demanding-answers/

Geoghegan, T. (2013, October 28). *Why is broadband more expensive in the US?*. Retrieved June 13, 2017, from http://www.bbc.com/news/magazine-24528383

Gibbs, S. (2016, January 28). *How much are you worth to Facebook?*. Retrieved May 23, 2017, from https://www.theguardian.com/technology/2016/jan/28/how-much-are-you-worth-to-facebook

Goldman, D. (2014, August 29). *Slow Comcast speeds were costing Netflix customers*. Retrieved May 23, 2017, from http://money.cnn.com/2014/08/29/technology/netflix-comcast

Goodin, D. (2014, January 30). *Ukrainian police use cellphones to track protesters, court order shows*. Retrieved January 8, 2017, from https://arstechnica.com/tech-policy/2014/01/ukrainian-police-use-cellphones-to-track-protestors-court-order-shows/

Greenberg, A. (2012, June 22). *CEO Of Internet Provider Sonic.net: We Delete User Logs After Two Weeks. Your Internet Provider Should, Too*. Retrieved May 23, 2017, from https://www.forbes.com/sites/andygreenberg/2012/06/22/ceo-of-internet-provider-sonic-net-we-delete-user-logs-after-two-weeks-your-internet-provider-should-too/

This is an opinion piece from a Forbes Contributor and should be read as such. However, the information about Sonic.net and the record keeping of other ISPs is accurate, and this article provides a good breakdown of them.

Gunaratna, S. (2016, May 9). *Report: Facebook manipulates what's "trending"*. Retrieved April 12, 2017, from http://www.cbsnews.com/news/report-trending-on-facebook-not-what-you-think-curators-manipulate-news/

Head, B. (2014, October 7). *MasterCard to access Facebook user data*. Retrieved January 3, 2017, from http://www.smh.com.au/it-pro/business-it/mastercard-to-access-facebook-user-data-20141006-10qrqy.html

Helper, S. (2014, December 16). *How Much Competition Exists Among ISPs*. Retrieved December 22, 2016, from http://www.esa.doc.gov/under-secretary-blog/how-much-competition-exists-among-isps

Hill, K. (2014, June 28). *Facebook Manipulated 689,003 Users' Emotions For Science*. Retrieved May 27, 2017, from https://www.forbes.com/sites/kashmirhill/2014/06/28/facebook-manipulated-689003-users-emotions-for-science/

Horrigan, B. (2016, March 22). 6. *Adults with tech-access tools are more likely to be lifelong learners and rely on the internet to pursue knowledge*. Retrieved April 23, 2017, from http://www.pewinternet.org/2016/03/22/adults-with-tech-access-tools-are-more-likely-to-be-lifelong-learners-and-rely-on-the-internet-to-pursue-knowledge/

How Netflix Works With ISPs Around the Globe to Deliver a Great Viewing Experience. (2016, March 17). Retrieved May 23,

2017, from https://media.netflix.com/en/company-blog/how-netflix-works-with-isps-around-the-globe-to-deliver-a-great-viewing-experience

[Institute for Local Self-Reliance]. (2015, July 8). *Gig City Sandy: Home of the $60 Gig* [Video file]. Retrieved January 12, 2017, from https://youtu.be/fBztjr2uCzg

Jameson. (2016, June 23). *How Much Does Data Really Cost an ISP?*. Retrieved January 10, 2017, from https://www.newamerica.org/oti/policy-papers/the-cost-of-connectivity-2014/

Kang, C. (2009, October 20). *AT&T lobbyist asks employees, their families and friends to protest net neutrality rules*. Retrieved May 1, 2017, from http://voices.washingtonpost.com/posttech/2009/10/att_lobbyist_asks_employees_th.html

Kang, C. (2017, March 23). *Congress Moves to Strike Internet Privacy Rules From Obama Era*. Retrieved May 1, 2017, from https://www.nytimes.com/2017/03/23/technology/congress-moves-to-strike-internet-privacy-rules-from-obama-era.html

Kastrenakes, J. (2014, September 16). *FCC received a total of 3.7 million comments on net neutrality*. Retrieved May 18, 2017, from https://www.theverge.com/2014/9/16/6257887/fcc-net-neutrality-3-7-million-comments-made

Kastrenakes, J. (2015, March 12). *These are the FCC's full rules for protecting net neutrality*. Retrieved May 23, 2017, from http://www.theverge.com/2015/3/12/8116237/net-neutrality-rules-open-internet-order-released

Kastrenakes, J. (2017, May 24). *2.6 million comments in, the FCC has changed almost nothing about its net neutrality proposal.* Retrieved June 2, 2017, from https://www.theverge.com/2017/5/24/15682240/fcc-net-neutrality-proposal-sees-few-changes

Kushnick, B. (2015). *The book of broken promises: $400 billion broadband scandal & free the net.* New York: New Networks Institute.

Lardinois, F. (2012, November 07). *Report: North American Internet Data Usage Up 120% In The Last Year, Netflix Still Responsible For 33% Of Peak Traffic.* Retrieved May 23, 2017, from https://techcrunch.com/2012/11/07/report-u-s-internet-data-usage-up-120-percent/

Lawler, R. (2015, January 16). *Sprint breaks ranks with other ISPs on net neutrality.* Retrieved May 23, 2017, from https://www.engadget.com/2015/01/16/sprint-net-neutrality-title-ii-is-ok/

Lee, T. (2012, July 03). *Verizon: net neutrality violates our free speech rights.* Retrieved June 18, 2017, from https://arstechnica.com/tech-policy/2012/07/verizon-net-neutrality-violates-our-free-speech-rights/

Lewis, D. (2014, May 20). *Verizon Details VoLTE Rollout Plans.* Retrieved May 23, 2017, from https://www.verizonwireless.com/news/article/2014/05/verizon-wireless-volte-national-rollout-plans.html

Liptak, A. (2007, September 27). *Verizon Blocks Messages of Abortion Rights Group.* Retrieved May 25, 2017, from http://www.nytimes.com/2007/09/27/us/27verizon.html

Liptak, A. (2012, June 21). *Supreme Court Rejects F.C.C. Fines for Indecency*. Retrieved May 23, 2017, from http://www.nytimes.com/2012/06/22/business/media/ justices-reject-indecency-fines-on-narrow-grounds.html? _r=0

Lobbying Spending Database Telecom Services, 2017. (n.d.). Retrieved May 23, 2017, from http://www.opensecrets.org/lobby/indusclient.php? id=B09

Lohr, S. (2012, February 29). *Impatient Web Users Flee Slow-Loading Sites*. Retrieved May 23, 2017, from http://www.nytimes.com/2012/03/01/technology/impa tient-web-users-flee-slow-loading-sites.html

Lutz, A. (2012, June 14). *These 6 Corporations Control 90% Of The Media In America*. Retrieved May 23, 2017, from http://www.businessinsider.com/these-6-corporations-control-90-of-the-media-in-america-2012-6

Masnick, M. (2013, January 23). *Cable Industry Finally Admits That Data Caps Have Nothing To Do With Congestion*. Retrieved January 10, 2017, from https://www.techdirt.com/articles/20130118/174252217 36/cable-industry-finally-admits-that-data-caps-have-nothing-to-do-with-congestion.shtml

Masnick, M. (2014, April 5). *Verizon Knows You're A Sucker: Takes Taxpayer Subsidies For Broadband, Doesn't Deliver, Lobbies To Drop Requirements*. Retrieved May 23, 2017, from https://www.techdirt.com/articles/20140424/061850270 14/verizon-knows-youre-sucker-takes-taxpayer-subsidies-broadband-doesnt-deliver-lobbies-to-drop-requirements.shtml

Matsa, K., & Lu, K. (2016, September 14). *10 facts about the changing digital news landscape.* Retrieved May 23, 2017, from http://www.pewresearch.org/fact-tank/2016/09/14/facts-about-the-changing-digital-news-landscape/

McAfee. (2015). *The Hidden Data Economy.* Santa Clara, CA: McFarland, C., Paget, F., & Samani, R.

McAlone, N. (2015, December 7). *This stat shows how thoroughly Netflix is crushing its competitors.* Retrieved May 26, 2017, from http://www.businessinsider.com/netflix-bandwidth-usage-compared-to-competitors-2015-12

McCullagh, D. (2008, August 20). *FCC formally rules Comcast's throttling of BitTorrent was illegal.* Retrieved June 18, 2017, from https://www.cnet.com/news/fcc-formally-rules-comcasts-throttling-of-bittorrent-was-illegal/

McGee, J. (2015, September 29). *AT&T drops fiber prices to Google Fiber levels.* Retrieved December 22, 2016, from http://www.tennessean.com/story/money/2015/09/29/t-drops-fiber-prices-google-fiber-levels/73023434/

McGee, J. (2016, June 14). *Chattanooga mayor: Gigabit speed internet helped revive city.* Retrieved May 18, 2017, from http://www.tennessean.com/story/money/2016/06/14/chattanooga-mayor-gigabit-speed-internet-helped-revive-city/85843196/

Merchant, B. (2013, August 19). *26 Million Americans Can't Afford the Internet.* Retrieved May 23, 2017, from https://motherboard.vice.com/en_us/article/26-million-americans-cant-afford-the-internet

Miranda, L. (2013, December 6). *Verizon, the FCC and What*

You Need to Know About Net Neutrality. Retrieved May 23, 2017, from https://www.thenation.com/article/verizon-fcc-and-what-you-need-know-about-net-neutrality/

Mirani, L. (2015, February 09). *Millions of Facebook users have no idea they're using the internet*. Retrieved May 23, 2017, from https://qz.com/333313/milliions-of-facebook-users-have-no-idea-theyre-using-the-internet/

Mitchell, A., Gottfried, J., Barthel, M., & Shearer, E. (2016, July 7). *The Modern News Consumer*. Retrieved December 17, 2016, from http://www.journalism.org/2016/07/07/pathways-to-news/

Morran, C. (2017, May 9). *Verizon Is Now Flat-Out Lying About Efforts To Kill Net Neutrality*. Retrieved May 10, 2017, from https://consumerist.com/2017/05/01/verizon-is-now-flat-out-lying-about-efforts-to-kill-net-neutrality/

Murphy, M. (2017, March 5). *Google Home, the search giant's virtual assistant, is sharing fake news*. Retrieved June 4, 2017, from https://qz.com/924975/google-goog-home-is-sharing-fake-news/

Noland, J. (2017, June 9). *8 members of Congress are leading the charge to repeal Net Neutrality. Here's exactly how much money they have received from Comcast, Verizon, and other ISPs*. Retrieved June 20, 2017, from https://act.represent.us/sign/Net_neutrality_contributions/

Nordrum, A. (2017, January 18). *Is Net Neutrality Good or Bad for Innovation?*. Retrieved May 27, 2017 from http://spectrum.ieee.org/tech-talk/telecom/internet/does-net-neutrality-help-or-harm-innovation

Oberhaus, D. (2017, May 25). *Dead People Are Posting Anti-Net Neutrality Comments to the FCC Website*. Retrieved May 26, 2017, from https://motherboard.vice.com/en_us/article/dead-people-are-posting-anti-net-neutrality-comments-to-the-fcc-website

Page, J. (2012, August 1). *Legislative audit blasts UTOPIA's planning, use of bond funds*. Retrieved May 30, 2017, from http://www.deseretnews.com/article/865559875/Legislative-audit-blasts-UTOPIAs-planning-use-of-bond-funds.html?pg=all

Rainie, L., & D'Vera C. (2014, September 19). *Census: Computer ownership, internet connection varies widely across U.S*. Retrieved January 3, 2017, from http://www.pewresearch.org/fact-tank/2014/09/19/census-computer-ownership-internet-connection-varies-widely-across-u-s/

Reardon, M. (2008, June 18). *AT&T and Verizon say FCC Net neutrality principles work*. Retrieved May 23, 2017, from https://www.cnet.com/news/at-t-and-verizon-say-fcc-net-neutrality-principles-work/

Reardon, M. (2015, March 26). *Sprint CEO: Without Net neutrality rules, we're toast*. Retrieved May 29, 2017, from https://www.cnet.com/news/sprint-ceo-without-net-neutrality-rules-we-are-toast/

Reardon, M. (2017, February 7). *Democrats promise to fight threats to kill net neutrality*. Retrieved May 8, 2017, from https://www.cnet.com/news/democrats-promise-to-fight-threats-to-kill-net-neutrality/

Rep. No. FCC-00290 (2000).

Schatz, A. (2014, July 03). *Where's Google in the Net Neutrality Fight?*. Retrieved May 23, 2017, from http://www.recode.net/2014/7/3/11628552/wheres-google-in-the-net-neutrality-fight

Scott, M. (2014, October 8). *Tim Berners-Lee, Web Creator, Defends Net Neutrality*. Retrieved June 1, 2017, from https://bits.blogs.nytimes.com/2014/10/08/tim-berners-lee-web-creator-defends-net-neutrality/

Selyukh, A. (2016, October 28). *Big Media Companies And Their Many Brands — In One Chart*. Retrieved May 23, 2017, from http://www.npr.org/sections/alltechconsidered/2016/10/28/499495517/big-media-companies-and-their-many-brands-in-one-chart

Shein, E. (2012, September 21). *AT&T Blocks FaceTime, Net Neutrality Complaint Filed*. Retrieved May 11, 2017, from www.informationweek.com/consumer/atandt-blocks-facetime-net-neutrality-complaint-filed/d/d-id/1106448

Snider, M. (2017, June 1). *Net neutrality opponents agree: FCC fake comments are a problem*. Retrieved June 4, 2017, from https://www.usatoday.com/story/tech/talkingtech/2017/06/01/fake-net-neutrality-comments-found-both-sides-fcc-issue/102389708/

SOPA/PIPA: Internet Blacklist Legislation. (n.d.). Retrieved June 04, 2017, from https://www.eff.org/issues/coica-internet-censorship-and-copyright-bill

Sottek, T. (2016, December 02). *This insane example from the FCC shows why AT&T and Verizon's zero rating schemes are a*

racket. Retrieved May 23, 2017, from
http://www.theverge.com/2016/12/2/13820498/att-verizon-fcc-zero-rating-gonna-have-a-bad-time

Summers, N. (2017, April 21). *Canada strengthens net neutrality with zero-rating crackdown*. Retrieved May 28, 2017, from
https://www.engadget.com/2017/04/21/canada-zero-rating-quebecor-videotron/

Sydell, L. (2015, February 27). *Long Before Net Neutrality, Rules Leveled The Landscape For Phone Services*. Retrieved May 23, 2017, from
http://www.npr.org/sections/alltechconsidered/2015/02/27/389318714/fcc-votes-along-party-lines-for-net-neutrality

Szoka, B., Starr, M., & Henke, J. (2013, July 16). *Don't Blame Big Cable. It's Local Governments That Choke Broadband Competition*. Retrieved February 8, 2017, from
https://www.wired.com/2013/07/we-need-to-stop-focusing-on-just-cable-companies-and-blame-local-government-for-dismal-broadband-competition/

The ISP Column, April 2014 - RIP Net Neutrality. (2014, April 25). Retrieved April 3, 2017, from
http://www.internetsociety.org/publications/isp-column-april-2014-rip-net-neutrality

Turmelle, L. (2017, January 13). *WFSB pulled from Optimum lineup in 24 Connecticut towns*. Retrieved March 1, 2017, from
http://www.registercitizen.com/article/RC/20170113/NEWS/170119786

Watson, L. (2017, May 11). *An ISP Shill Group Is Trotting Out Misleading Google Ads About Net Neutrality*. Retrieved May

23, 2017, from http://gizmodo.com/an-isp-shill-group-is-trotting-out-misleading-google-ad-1795126118

Wehner, M. (2015, April 15). *Google Fiber is succeeding and cable companies are starting to feel the pressure*. Retrieved December 23, 2016, from http://www.businessinsider.com/google-fiber-is-succeeding-and-cable-companies-are-starting-to-feel-the-pressure-2015-4

Weissberger, A. (2016, December 07). *Verizon to test 5G "wireless fiber" for Internet & TV in Spring 2017*. Retrieved May 23, 2017, from http://techblog.comsoc.org/2016/12/07/verizon-to-test-5g-wireless-fiber-for-internet-tv-in-spring-2017/

Who Owns the Media?. (n.d.). Retrieved December 15, 2016, from http://www.freepress.net/ownership/chart

Wu, T. (2012). *The Master Switch: The Rise and Fall of Information Empires*. London: Atlantic.

Yang, J. (2009, May 10). *Google: A 'natural monopoly'?*. Retrieved July 1, 2017, from http://archive.fortune.com/2009/05/07/technology/yang_google.fortune/index.htm

Zhang, Y., Mao, Z. M., & Zhang, M. (2008, October). *Ascertaining the Reality of Network Neutrality Violation in Backbone ISPs*. In HotNets (pp. 121-126).